Paws and Praise Jesus
30 Devotions for Dog Lovers

By John B. McKissack

TABLE OF CONTENTS

- i -
The Rescue That Changed Everything

There has never been a day in my life when I didn't thank God for creating dogs. I say that without exaggeration. Dogs have been one of the greatest earthly gifts the Lord has ever placed in my life, living reminders of loyalty, joy, devotion, protection, and a kind of unconditional affection that feels like it was woven directly into their souls by the hand of God Himself.

Today, one of my greatest daily blessings is a little dog named Lottie. She is small, soft, bright-eyed, and full of a kind of gentle happiness that warms my heart even on the hardest days. Wherever I am, Lottie is close by, curled at my feet, following me from room to room, or watching me with those eyes that somehow say, "I love you, I trust you, and I'm glad you're here." I've come to realize that she isn't just my dog, she's one of my best friends. Her joy becomes my joy. Her devotion becomes my comfort. And the more time I spend with her, the more I understand that a dog is not "just a pet." They are a gift from God, a companion carefully designed to walk through life with us.

And Lottie is only here because of those who came before her, including one of the most faithful dogs I've ever known, a dog named Wee Dawg. He was loyal to the core. He loved deeply, protected fiercely, and stayed close no matter what. He was the kind of dog you don't forget, the kind who leaves a permanent pawprint on your heart. But Wee Dawg's story didn't start with him. It started with his father, and that's where this whole journey truly began.

Years ago, our family was searching for a missing dog. We had no intention of adopting another one. We were simply looking for the one we had lost. But God has a way of arranging moments we never expect, and that day, He arranged one that changed our lives forever.

As we walked through the pound, my eyes fell on a small,

starving puppy curled in the corner of a cold concrete kennel. His belly was swollen and distended from parasites. His ribs stuck out sharply through his thin skin. His fur was patchy, falling out in clumps from red mange, and his whole little body trembled with weakness. He tried to bark when he saw us, but no sound came out. He was too weak even to cry for help.

The worker looked at the puppy with sadness and said quietly, "You can try to rescue him if you want… but he probably won't make it."

Before I could respond, my little daughter, Christian, knelt beside the kennel. Her young heart saw not a dying dog, but a life worth saving. She looked up at me with pleading eyes and whispered, "Daddy, can we please try? Please?"

Everything in me wanted to say no. I was a grown man, thinking practically. I knew how far gone the puppy looked. I tried to explain to her gently that he was likely dying. I didn't want her heart to break. As I walked her toward the car, I kept telling myself we were doing the right thing.

But then, just as we reached the parking lot, the pound worker ran after us. She was out of breath, waving her hands, her face full of compassion and desperation.

"Please," she said, "please at least try to save him. No paperwork. No fee. Just take him. Give him a chance."

I looked at her face. I looked at the dying puppy in her arms. I looked down at my daughter's hopeful eyes filled with tears. And in that moment, I felt something shift inside me. I could almost hear the Holy Spirit whisper, "This is the one. Take him home."

So we did.

We named him Captain Ron, after the quirky movie character, because we figured every dog deserved a name filled with strength and adventure, even if he didn't look like either at the moment. That night, after researching red mange, I learned something that surprised me: there is no medical cure. The only way for the dog to survive is for its immune system to fight it off on its own.

So we made a decision: if his little immune system was going to have a chance, then we were going to give him everything he needed.

The best food.

The best vitamins.

The best minerals.

The best nutrients.

And more importantly, the best love.

We held him when he shook. We fed him gently. We cleaned his sores. We wrapped him in blankets. We prayed over him. We told him he was safe. We told him he was wanted. And day after day, that little dog fought with everything he had. Slowly, the mange receded. His fur began to grow back. His strength returned. His bark found its way out. And eventually, he became a healthy, handsome, energetic dog with a personality as big as the life he had been given.

And from Captain Ron came Wee Dawg, and from Wee Dawg came Lottie.

Three generations of joy.

Three generations of love.

Three reminders that a rescued life becomes a blessing that ripples through time.

Captain Ron should have died alone on a cold shelter floor, unseen and unloved. Instead, he became part of a family. And in saving him, something in us was saved too. Because rescuing that broken little dog reminded me of something powerful:

This is exactly what Jesus did for us.

We were spiritually sick, and He healed us.

We were unwanted by the world, and He chose us.

We were trapped in our sin, and He rescued us.

We were without hope, and He brought us home.

Captain Ron's story is the story of grace.

Wee Dawg's story is the story of faithfulness.

Lottie's story is the story of joy.

But beyond my own experiences, I believe dogs matter spiritually in a very real and beautiful way. God could have created the world without them. He could have filled creation with only practical creatures, animals to work, animals to feed us, animals to serve a purpose. But instead, He gave us dogs: companions capable of love, loyalty, forgiveness, and joy. Dogs aren't accidental creations, they are intentional reflections of God's heart toward us.

A dog's loyalty mirrors God's faithfulness.

A dog's excitement at our return echoes heaven's joy when we come near.

A dog's unconditional love reminds us of grace.

A dog's desire to walk beside us looks like discipleship.

A dog's ability to forgive instantly reflects the mercy of God.

A dog's trust in its master teaches us how to trust in our Savior.

Dogs preach a silent sermon every day. They show us how to love without hesitation, how to forgive without remembering the wound, and how to stay close to the one who cares for us. They remind us that presence is more important than perfection. Their affection is pure, uncomplicated, and sincere, qualities our faith often lacks but desperately needs.

In a world full of distractions, anxieties, and spiritual noise, God gave us dogs as gentle reminders of His nearness. They are, in many ways, little reflections of His steadfast heart, always ready to comfort, always ready to rejoice, always ready to follow, always ready to love. Dogs invite us into a deeper spiritual truth: that life is richer, fuller, and more peaceful when we stay close to the One who loves us most.

This book, Paws and Praise Jesus, is my chance to share those stories with you, and to celebrate the God who created dogs as a reflection of His loving heart. Dogs are living parables of loyalty, love, forgiveness, and devotion. They remind us daily of what God is like, and of the kind of hearts we are called to have.

So as you read these devotions, may your heart be warmed,

your faith strengthened, and your spirit lifted and may you see what I see every day. God gave us dogs to be illustrations of His tender, unconditional love.

- 1 -
Tail-Wagging Joy

Paws and Open Your Heart

There is nothing in the world quite like the joy of a dog who loves you.

You don't even have to say a word.

Somehow, they just know.

Long before your key ever touches the lock, they hear your car, your footsteps, the familiar rhythm of your daily return. Their ears perk up, the tail starts its soft thump-thump-thump, and before you even cross the threshold, they're already smiling with their whole body.

Dogs don't do "polite greetings."

They launch themselves into joy.

The moment you walk in, the tail becomes a blur, one of those full-body, almost-lose-their-balance wags. Their paws dance, their eyes brighten, and sometimes their excitement is so overwhelming they can't help but bounce in place like a little kid who can't contain happiness.

And they do it every single time.

You can leave for five minutes to check the mail…and when you walk back inside, they act like you've returned from a voyage across the ocean.

To them, your presence is always worth celebrating.

Every greeting is a homecoming.

Every return is a reunion.

It doesn't matter what kind of day they've had.

It doesn't matter how long you've been gone.

It doesn't matter if they're tired, or older now, or their hips ache a little.

When they see you, something inside of them lights up.

Dogs love with this wild, uncomplicated enthusiasm, this pure, unfiltered happiness that doesn't ask questions or hold back. They don't wait to see if you're in a good mood, or check whether you brought treats, or measure if you've earned their affection that day. They just love you because... you're theirs.

A dog will follow you from room to room, not because they're needy, but because being near you is their favorite place to be. They'll curl up at your feet, or sit next to the bathtub, or lay down by the couch, anywhere you are, they want to be too. Their quiet presence is its own kind of devotion.

And when you leave the room?

They'll wait.

Some wait by the window, watching the driveway like a little guardian.

Some wait by the door, chin resting on their paws, listening for you.

Some pace in tiny circles, unsure where you vanished to but hopeful that you'll return soon.

And the moment you come back?

There it is again, that whole-body, can't-hold-it-in, tail-wagging explosion of joy.

It doesn't fade.

It doesn't tire.

It doesn't become routine.

To them, you remain the best part of their world.

A dog's joy is not subtle.

It's not careful or fearful or measured.

It's loud and energetic and wholehearted.

It's love that leaps before it looks.

It's joy that spills over the moment you appear.

And maybe that's why dog lovers feel something deep in their chest when their dog runs to greet them, it's like the dog is saying with every wag, every bounce, every happy sound:

"You matter. I'm glad you're here. My day is better because of you."

And the truth is...

if you've ever had a dog meet you at the door like that,

you know exactly what it feels like to be loved without limits.

Scripture to Sink Your Teeth Into

Psalm 42:1–2
As the deer pants for streams of water,
so my soul pants for you, my God.
My soul thirsts for God, for the living God.
When can I go and meet with God?

Lesson To Chew On
-
Loving Jesus With That Same Tail-Wagging Joy

There is something deeply humbling about the way a dog loves. Dogs don't love halfway or cautiously. They don't measure their affection or wonder whether they should hold back. They love with their whole being, ears up, tail wagging, eyes bright, heart wide open. They are ready to run toward you the moment they sense you are near. And somehow, as simple as it seems, there is a gentle truth in that kind of love that speaks to the soul.

Because in a small, earthly way, the love a dog shows its owner is a glimpse of the love our hearts were created to have toward Jesus. Dogs don't complicate love or wait for a perfect moment. They love because of who you are to them. Their joy is tied to your presence, not your performance. Their happiness wakes up the second you walk into the room. And maybe, just maybe, that is a picture of the kind of joyful, eager love God desires from us.

Psalm 42 gives words to that longing: "My soul pants longingly for You… my inner self thirsts for the living God." This is the language of a heart that doesn't love Jesus out of routine but out of desire. It's the heart that perks up at His voice, that feels at home in His presence, and that goes searching for Him when He seems far away. It's the heart that quietly says, "Lord, where You are is where I want to be."

That kind of love doesn't happen instantly. It grows the same way a dog's devotion grows, through time spent together, trust built across days and years, a sense of safety and belonging that deepens with every moment in His presence. A dog follows its owner from room to room because it has learned that where you are, there is comfort and joy. And when our hearts learn the same thing about Jesus, love begins to flow naturally and wholeheartedly.

This is not a love driven by duty or pressure. It is not motivated by guilt, fear, or empty ritual. It is a love that runs, a love that longs, a love that finds joy simply because the Master is near. Jesus does not pull back when He sees you coming. He does not stand still and wait for you to prove yourself worthy. He meets you with compassion, just as the father ran to the prodigal son, and just as your dog runs to meet you at the door every single day.

So today, let your heart approach Jesus with that same simple, honest affection. Come to Him quickly, gladly, joyfully, without hesitation or shame. Come to Him because He is your peace, your comfort, your safety, and the One who loves you without limit. Let your soul move toward Him the way a beloved dog moves toward its owner, full of trust, full of joy, full of love. Because Jesus is worthy of that kind of love, and your heart was created to give it.

Curl Up Close and Pray

Lord Jesus,

Thank You for loving me with a love that is patient, faithful, and constant.
Thank You for drawing near to me even when I feel far away.
Today, I ask You to grow in my heart the kind of love that longs for Your presence. Teach me to come to You quickly and joyfully, without hesitation or fear. Help me to seek You with the same eager devotion that a loyal dog shows toward the one it loves, simple, honest, and wholehearted.
Let my soul wake up to Your nearness.
Let my heart cling to You.
Let my joy be found not in what happens around me but in the fact that You are here.
Where You are is where I want to be, Lord. Lead me closer to You, teach me to love You more deeply, and fill me with the kind of affection that runs toward You every day of my life.
Thank You for welcoming me, embracing me, and finding joy in my returning.
Make my heart steady, my love sincere, and my devotion real.
I love You, Jesus.
Help me love You even more.

In Jesus' name I pray,
Amen.

- 2 -
Sit, Stay, Trust

Paws and Open Your Heart

Every dog owner knows that "sit" and "stay" are two of the most basic commands. Simple words, short syllables... yet somehow the hardest for a dog to learn, because they require something deeper than instinct. They require trust.

At first, a young dog doesn't understand why they should sit still.

They wiggle, they inch forward, they crane their neck to see if you're moving.

Their tail sweeps the floor like a metronome of excitement.

Everything inside them says, "Let me run to you! Let me get closer! Let me do something!"

But little by little, with gentle training and patient love, they begin to understand. The tone of your voice. The calm in your eyes. The assurance in your posture. They learn that when you ask them to sit, you're not withholding something good, you're preparing them to receive it.

And when you ask them to stay, you're not abandoning them, you're teaching them to trust that you will return.

You can see it in the way a dog waits, muscles poised and ready, ears perked and trembling, eyes fixed on your every move. Their whole body is a question:

"Is it time yet? Can I come now? Are you still here?"

And still, they stay.

And sometimes, there's that moment, a soft whine, a little shuffle, the paw that creeps forward just an inch, because they're trying so hard to obey even while everything in them longs to move. Because obedience, for a dog, isn't about perfection. It's about heart. It's about wanting to get it right for the one they love.

Then comes the best part, the moment you say, "Okay!" or "Come!"

Suddenly, all that pent-up energy bursts like a dam breaking.

They leap forward with joy, tail spinning like a rotor, eyes shining because the wait is over.

The trust was worth it.

You kept your promise.

You called them back to your side.

There's beauty in that moment,

the way they listen,

the way they let go,

the way they stay still even when they'd rather run,

just because you asked them to.

And there's a quiet, powerful truth hidden inside that simple act:

A dog doesn't sit and stay because they understand the reason.

They sit and stay because they trust the one who asked them to.

Their obedience isn't about logic,

it's about love.

They don't need the full explanation.

They don't need the whole map.

They don't need to know what comes next.

All they need is your voice...

and the assurance that you are good.

If you've ever watched a dog sit, stay, and wait with anxious anticipation...

you've witnessed one of the most tender pictures of trust that creation has to offer.

Because behind those shining eyes and twitching ears, a dog carries a heart that says:

"I don't understand everything... but I know you.

And because I know you, I trust you."

And somehow, with all their simplicity and innocence,

dogs show us what steady, eager, loyal trust looks like,
not trust in the situation...
but trust in the One who leads.

Scripture to Sink Your Teeth Into

Psalm 37:3–7 (AMP)
3 Trust [rely on and have confidence] in the Lord and do good;
Dwell in the land and feed [securely] on His faithfulness.
4 Delight yourself in the Lord,
And He will give you the desires and petitions of your heart.
5 Commit your way to the Lord;
Trust in Him also and He will do it.
6 He will make your righteousness (your pursuit of right standing with God) shine like the light,
And your judgment like the shining of the noonday sun.
7 Be still before the Lord; wait patiently for Him and entrust yourself to Him...

Lesson To Chew On

Learning to Trust the Master Who Says "Sit" and "Stay"
Trusting Jesus is often far more like a dog's obedience than we realize. Not because we are simple, but because trust itself is simple. It isn't complicated or intellectual at its core, it is relational. It is built on knowing the One who speaks. And sometimes, the greatest tests of trust come when God asks us to do the spiritual equivalent of what a dog struggles with the most:

Sit. Stay.

When God whispers, "Be still," everything inside us often wants to move. We want to make something happen. Fix something. Change something. Run toward something. We want to see progress, answers, resolution, anything but stillness. Sitting feels inactive. Staying feels unproductive. Waiting feels like we're falling behind.

But just like a loving owner who trains a dog, God's commands are never about withholding good from us. They are about preparing our hearts to receive it.

A dog doesn't understand why "sit" matters.

They don't know the reasons, only the voice.

And so much of our faith is the same way.

We don't always understand the why, but we recognize the One who speaks.

Sometimes God says, "Sit." Not as a punishment, but as protection.

Sometimes He says, "Stay." Not to deny us movement, but to deepen our trust.

Sometimes He holds us in place, not because He has forgotten us, but because He is setting the stage for what comes next.

Dogs wait with their whole hearts, ears forward, body trembling, eyes fixed, longing to run the moment you say the word. And while they wait, they trust that your command is good. They trust that the release will come. They trust that you are not gone forever, you are simply asking them to hold still until the moment is right.

Psalm 37 echoes that same truth:

"Be still before the Lord; wait patiently for Him and entrust yourself to Him…"

Entrust yourself.

That's what "stay" really means.

It means believing that God's timing is not late.

It means trusting that His plan is better than our sprinting.

It means holding still even when our hearts are twitching to run ahead.

And when God says, "Okay, come," oh, the joy that follows!

Just like the dog who leaps forward the moment the waiting ends, our hearts burst with relief and celebration when God finally opens the door and releases what He's been preparing.

The wait wasn't wasted.

The stillness wasn't pointless.

The command wasn't punishment.

It was love.

It was training.

It was trust being built in the quiet places of obedience.

And maybe that's the truth a dog teaches us better than anything else:

We don't have to understand everything God asks of us,

we just have to trust the One who asks.

Because when the heart learns to sit and stay at Jesus' command…

it will run with far greater joy when He finally says, "Come."

Curl Up Close and Pray

Lord Jesus,

Thank You for being patient with me when I struggle to slow down, to wait, or to hold still in the moments You ask me to trust. You know how easily my heart becomes restless, how quickly I want to move ahead, fix what I cannot fix, or run toward answers that aren't ready yet. And yet, in Your kindness, You teach me, just as a loving master teaches a beloved dog, that waiting is not punishment. It is protection. It is preparation. It is love.

Help me to sit when You say sit.

Help me to stay when You say stay.

And help me to trust that You are good in every command You give me.

Quiet my racing thoughts.

Steady my anxious heart.

Let me rest in Your presence without fear or frustration.

Teach me to believe, not just with my mind, but with my whole being, that You have my best in mind even when I don't understand the timing.

Give me the kind of trusting heart that leans into Your voice, the kind that stays close until You call me forward, the kind that waits with hope instead of worry. And when the moment comes that You say "Go," let me run with joy, knowing that You have released me into the very thing You prepared for me.

Thank You for loving me enough to guide me, to teach me, and to lead me step by step.

I entrust myself to You today, Lord.

Strengthen my trust.

Deepen my obedience.

And draw me closer to Your heart as I learn to sit, stay, and trust in Your perfect timing.

Amen.

- 3 -

Come When Called

Paws and Open Your Heart

Every dog owner knows the moment. You step outside, call your dog's name, and for a split second the whole world feels suspended, because everything depends on how they respond. Will they listen this time? Will they come running? Or will they pause, glance back, and decide whether something else is more interesting than you?

A dog's response to being called is its own small drama, revealing so much about the relationship between you and the one you love.

Sometimes, they come instantly.

No hesitation, no wandering, no weighing their options.

They hear your voice and something inside them leaps.

Their ears perk, their tail flicks once, and then,

here they come.

Charging across the yard.

Barreling over fallen sticks, kicking up leaves behind them.

Eyes locked on you like you're the brightest spot in their world.

Those moments make your heart swell. There's a kind of purity in the way they run toward you, as if returning to you is the only thing that makes sense. You call... and they come. Not out of fear, not out of duty, but out of joy.

But there are other moments too, the ones dog owners know all too well.

You call their name, and they freeze.

A squirrel darts along the fence line.

A smell in the grass suddenly becomes irresistible.

A butterfly zigzags just a little too close.

And you can practically see the wheels turning inside their head:

"Do I come now?

Or do I chase that thing over there just for a second?"

And before you know it, they're running the exact opposite direction of your voice.

So you call again.

A little louder this time.

A little firmer.

A little more desperate.

And still, they're enthralled by whatever distraction stole their attention.

But even then,

even after darting after a squirrel, or lingering too long by the fence, or pretending they don't hear you,

there eventually comes a moment when they turn.

Their head lifts.

Their ears swivel back toward you.

Their eyes soften.

And their feet begin to move.

First a trot.

Then a canter.

Then a full-on sprint back into your arms.

And when they finally reach you, panting, tail spinning, body leaning into your legs, it's as if the disobedient detour never happened. They're just glad to be home. And you're glad they came when they heard your voice, even if it took a few extra calls.

Because no matter what distracted them…

no matter how far they ran…

no matter how long they lingered…

your voice still reached the place where their heart answered most.

And inside that reunion is something indescribably sweet,

the reminder that dogs, for all their imperfections and distractions, still know where they belong.

They still know who they love.

They still know the sound of the one who calls their name.

A dog may wander, but when they finally come running, ears flapping, paws pounding, joy spilling out of them, you see the truth:

They came because they know your voice.

They came because they trust your call.

They came because home is wherever you are.

Scripture to Sink Your Teeth Into

John 10:2–4, 14, 27–28 (AMP)

2 But he who enters by the door is the shepherd of the sheep [the protector and provider].

3 The doorkeeper opens the gate for this man, and the sheep hear his voice and pay attention to it. And knowing that they listen, he calls his own sheep by name and leads them out.

4 When he has brought all his own sheep outside, he walks on ahead of them, and the sheep follow him because they know his voice.

14 I am the Good Shepherd, and I know [without any doubt] those who are My own and My own know Me [have a deep, personal relationship with Me],

27 The sheep that are My own hear My voice and listen to Me; I know them, and they follow Me.

28 And I give them eternal life, and they will never, ever [by any means] perish; and no one will ever snatch them out of My hand.

Lesson To Chew On

Learning to Respond When Jesus Calls Your Name

There is a sacred tenderness in the way Jesus calls us. He doesn't shout to frighten us or force us into obedience. He calls the way a loving shepherd calls His sheep, gently, personally, by name. Not with pressure, but with presence. Not with fear, but with love. And so much of our walk with the Lord can be understood through that simple image: hearing His voice… and choosing to come when He calls.

Dogs have this remarkable ability to recognize the voice of the one they love. They can pick your tone out of a hundred sounds in the backyard. They know your footsteps, your whistle, your rhythm, your presence. And when their heart is in the right place, they come running, not because they are afraid of what will happen if they don't, but because they are drawn to you.

Spiritually, we're not that different.

Jesus is always calling.

Calling us closer.

Calling us out of old habits.

Calling us away from distractions that steal our time and peace.

Calling us to deeper trust, deeper rest, deeper belonging.

But often, like dogs in a yard full of squirrels, our attention darts everywhere except toward Him. We hear His voice faintly at first, a nudge, a pull, a whisper... and part of us knows we should turn. But our feet keep wandering. Something else seems interesting. Something else seems urgent. Something else seems easier.

And still, Jesus calls.

Not once.

Not twice.

But again and again with the persistence of love.

He doesn't give up when we run the wrong direction. He doesn't stop calling because we hesitated. He doesn't fold His arms and walk away because we chose a distraction over obedience. His voice keeps reaching for us, steady, patient, full of grace.

And when we finally turn...

when our heart swivels back toward Him...

when we recognize His voice above all the noise...

everything changes.

Like a dog who suddenly remembers where home is, our soul begins to move,

slow at first, then faster, then with full-hearted conviction.

We come because we know His voice.

We come because we trust His heart.

We come because home is wherever He is.

John 10 tells us plainly:

"My sheep hear My voice... and they follow Me."

That is the essence of discipleship, not understanding every detail, not having everything figured out, but simply responding to the One who loves us. Hearing. Turning. Coming.

And the moment we draw near, Jesus meets us with the same joy a dog shows when the one they love walks through the door, except infinitely deeper, infinitely stronger, infinitely purer. There is no scolding, no shame, no lecture about where we wandered off to. Just the open arms of a Savior who has been calling our name the whole time.

The truth is, the Christian life is not about never getting distracted.

It's about learning to come quickly when Jesus calls.

It's about recognizing His voice above all others.

It's about trusting that no matter how far we wandered, His call is always an invitation home.

Because the One who calls you is the One who loves you.

And the heart that learns to come when Jesus speaks will find itself running into a love that never fails, never fades, and never stops calling your name.

Curl Up Close and Pray

Lord Jesus,

Thank You for being the kind of Savior who calls me by name. Thank You for speaking with love instead of force, gentleness instead of pressure, and patience instead of frustration. Your voice is the safest sound my soul will ever hear, and I want to learn how to recognize it more clearly every day.

Help me listen when You call.

Help me turn when I've wandered.

Help me come quickly, willingly, and joyfully into Your presence.

Lord, I confess that sometimes I get distracted. My heart chases lesser things. My attention wanders. My feet drift in directions You never meant for me to go. But thank You that You never stop calling me home. Thank You that Your voice doesn't give up on me, doesn't grow weary of reaching for me, and doesn't hesitate to welcome me back.

Teach me to love Your voice more than anything that competes for my attention.

Teach me to run toward You the moment I sense Your calling.

Teach me to trust that where You are is always where I belong.

Thank You for the grace that meets me every time I turn back.

Thank You for the joy that fills my heart when I draw near.

And thank You for being a Savior who never stops calling, never stops loving, and never stops leading me home.

I love You, Jesus.

Help me hear You.

Help me follow You.

Help me come when You call.

Amen.

- 4 -
The Dog at the Window

Paws and Open Your Heart

There's a certain kind of stillness only dog owners truly understand, the kind that happens when a dog plants itself at the window and waits. Not with impatience or irritation, but with a quiet, almost sacred expectancy. It's a posture filled with hope, loyalty, and something deeper: a love that believes the one they're waiting for will return.

Some dogs choose the same spot every day, a specific corner of the couch, a patch of worn carpet, a little sill warmed by sunlight. They climb up, settle in, and fix their gaze on whatever direction you last disappeared. Their eyes scan the road, the driveway, the sidewalk, watching for any sign of movement. There's a stillness in their body, but electricity in their heart.

They wait because they trust you.

They wait because they love you.

They wait because, in their world, you are worth waiting for.

Hours can pass, shadows can shift, the day can stretch on, and still, they watch. Occasionally their ears perk at the sound of a car door slamming down the street. Their head lifts when footsteps echo somewhere outside. Their tail gives a hopeful thump against the cushion as if to ask, "Is it you? Are you home?" And even when it's not, they never give up.

Sometimes they sigh and rest their head on their paws... but their eyes stay fixed on the window.

Sometimes they wander off for a drink of water...

but they always come back.

Because somewhere deep inside, they're certain of one thing:

You're coming home.

There's a quiet beauty in a dog's waiting, a faithfulness that doesn't fade with time. They don't check the clock or question your promise. They don't panic when it gets dark or assume the worst because the hours feel long. They don't let uncertainty steal their hope.

They simply wait.

Still.

Present.

Hopeful.

Believing that the door will eventually open, and the one they love will walk through it.

And when that moment finally arrives, when your car turns into the driveway, when your footsteps approach the door, something extraordinary happens. The dog who was still and silent transforms into a whirlwind of joy. Their tail becomes a blur, their paws tap the floor like a drum, their whole body quivers with excitement. Hope erupts into celebration.

But that explosion of joy was born in the quiet of waiting.

The love was already there.

The loyalty was already there.

The trust was already there.

All of it was sitting right by the window.

If you've ever watched a dog wait like that, with unwavering devotion and unshakable hope, you've witnessed a picture of something pure, love that watches, waits, and believes... even when the door hasn't opened yet.

Scripture to Sink Your Teeth Into

Psalm 130:5–6 (AMP)
5 I wait [patiently] for the Lord, my soul [expectantly] waits,
And in His word do I hope.
6 My soul waits for the Lord
More than the watchmen for the morning,
Yes, more than the watchmen for the morning.

Lesson To Chew On

Learning to Wait with Hopeful Eyes and a Trusting Heart

Waiting is one of the hardest things God ever asks us to do. Not because waiting itself is painful, but because waiting exposes what we truly believe about the One we're waiting for. When life slows down, when answers delay, when prayers linger in the silence, we discover whether our hope is fragile... or anchored. Whether our trust is shallow... or steadfast. Whether we believe Jesus is coming... or whether we doubt He remembers.

And strangely enough, a dog at a window teaches us something sacred about this.

A dog doesn't wait with panic.

They wait with expectation.

They don't fear abandonment.

They believe in return.

Their eyes stay fixed on the place you left because love assures them you will come back.

That kind of waiting is not desperate, it's devoted.

When the psalmist writes, "My soul waits for the Lord... more than watchmen for the morning," he is describing a posture of deep, steady hope. Watchmen weren't waiting to see if morning would come, they were waiting to see when it would break across the horizon. Morning was guaranteed; they simply had to watch for it.

And that's the kind of waiting God invites us into.

But most of us don't wait like watchmen. We wait like worriers.

We watch the clock instead of the horizon.

We imagine the worst instead of remembering the promise.

We hold our breath, afraid of what might not happen, instead of resting in what God has already said will happen.

Yet Scripture says, "In His word do I hope."

That means hope is not rooted in circumstance, it's rooted in His character.

It is not tied to outcomes, it is tied to the One who never fails.

If you've ever stood in a moment where everything in you longed for God to show up, you know how vulnerable waiting feels. Your heart feels exposed. Your fears whisper. Your doubts rattle around in the quiet.

And then God whispers back:

"Wait for Me. Keep looking. Keep trusting. I am coming."

A dog at the window doesn't move because they have proof; they stay because they have trust. Their world is small, but their faith is big. They believe in your goodness. They believe in your return. They believe in your love.

And maybe, just maybe, God is calling us to wait with that kind of expectancy.

To lift our eyes toward Him even when the path looks long.

To keep our hearts awake even when the silence stretches.

To stay by the window of hope, believing that the One we love is not distant, not delayed, not forgetful, but faithful.

Because when Jesus steps into the moment you've been waiting for,

when the prayer is answered,

when the breakthrough comes,

when the door finally opens,

all the quiet trust, all the steadfast watching, all the hope that held you up becomes joy overflowing.

Just like the dog who bursts into celebration the moment you walk through the door, your heart will overflow with gratitude when you see how faithfully God has kept His promise.

The waiting may be quiet, but it is never wasted.

Hope may feel still, but it is never empty.

And the One you're waiting for is always worth the watch.

Curl Up Close and Pray

Lord Jesus,

Thank You for being a God who is always faithful, always present, and always moving toward me, even when I cannot yet see it. Teach me to wait for You with the same kind of hopeful expectancy that a loyal dog shows while watching at the window. Let my heart learn to rest, to trust, and to look toward You with confidence instead of fear.

Sometimes waiting feels heavy.

Sometimes hope feels fragile.

Sometimes my thoughts drift toward doubt more quickly than toward faith.

But You, Lord, are steady.

You are true.

You are worth waiting for.

Help me fix my eyes on You, even when the days feel long or quiet.

Help me remember that Your timing is perfect, that Your promises are sure, and that Your presence is never far from me. Let my soul watch for You the way the psalmist described, trusting that You will come through, trusting that You hear me, trusting that You hold every part of my life in Your loving hands.

Give me peace in the waiting, strength in the silence, and hope that holds on even when my heart feels tired. And when the moment comes that You open the door, when You step into the situation I've been praying about, when Your answer finally arrives, let my joy overflow and my faith rise up in gratitude.

Thank You, Jesus, for being faithful.

Thank You for being near.

Thank You for being the God who always returns, always speaks, always keeps His word.

Teach me to wait with love, with trust, and with eyes lifted toward You.

Amen.

- 5 -
The Joy of Your Presence

Paws and Open Your Heart

There's a kind of joy a dog carries that feels almost sacred,
a joy that appears the moment you step into the room.
You don't have to bring a treat.
You don't have to say a word.
You don't even have to do anything special.
Your presence alone is enough.

Some dogs will lift their head from a nap the instant they hear you walk by, their tail tapping the floor in soft, sleepy rhythms. Others will trot across the room with that familiar thump-thump-thump of paws on hardwood, ready to lean their whole body into your leg just to feel close.

And some, oh, some, rejoice like it's the best moment of their day.

They spin in circles, wag so hard their whole backside wiggles, or press their head against your knee with an affection that seems to say:

"You're here. That's all I needed."
Dogs don't celebrate your accomplishments.
They celebrate you.
They don't care whether you succeeded or failed today.
They don't ask whether you came home tired or cheerful.
They don't watch for perfection.
They watch for presence.
To them, presence is the blessing.

Presence is the gift.

Presence is the joy.

Sometimes, all it takes is you sitting on the couch for your dog to immediately settle beside you, head on your lap, curled up against your leg, breathing slow and content just because you're near. The room hasn't changed, the day hasn't changed, the circumstances haven't changed, but your presence changed something inside their heart.

A dog doesn't need explanations.

They don't need reasons.

They don't need to understand the moment.

They only need you.

And perhaps one of the most beautiful things about a dog's love is this:

They enjoy being with you even in the ordinary moments.

No excitement required.

No big event.

No special occasion.

Just you, existing in the same space.

For a dog, joy isn't found in what you do.

Joy is found in who you are.

If you've ever sat with a dog resting peacefully beside you, their breathing slow and steady, their eyes half-closed in absolute contentment, you've felt the sweetness of a love that simply delights in nearness.

You didn't have to earn that moment.

You didn't have to perform for it.

You didn't have to prove anything.

You just had to be there.

And in that quiet, tender closeness,

in the way they relax into your presence,

the way their worry melts away,

the way their heart settles into peace,

you're reminded of something deeply true:

Sometimes the greatest joy comes not from what's happening around you, but from who you are close to.

A dog knows that.

A dog lives that.

And in their gentle, affectionate way, they show us a picture of what it means to find joy not in activity, but in relationship... not in doing, but in being... not in striving, but in simply being close to the one you love.

Scripture to Sink Your Teeth Into

Psalm 16:8–11 (AMP)

8 I have set the Lord continually before me;

Because He is at my right hand, I will not be shaken.

9 Therefore my heart is glad and my glory [my inner self] rejoices;

My body too will dwell confidently in safety,

10 For You will not abandon me to Sheol [the nether world, the place of the dead];

Nor will You allow Your Holy One to undergo decay.

11 You will show me the path of life;

In Your presence is fullness of joy;

In Your right hand there are pleasures forevermore.

Lesson To Chew On

Finding Joy Simply Because Jesus Is Near

There is something beautiful, and honestly, deeply instructive, about the way a dog finds joy in simple nearness. They don't need explanations. They don't need reasons. They don't need a special moment to feel content. Your presence, all by itself, is enough to fill their heart with warmth and rest.

And just like that, dogs quietly reveal a spiritual truth that many of us forget:

Joy isn't found in circumstances. Joy is found in presence.

Not in what is happening around us, but in who is with us.

In Psalm 16, David declares, "In Your presence is fullness of joy."

Not halfway joy.

Not temporary joy.

Not joy dependent on everything going right.

Fullness of joy.

The kind that doesn't crack under pressure, fade in hardship, or disappear in the quiet moments of life.

And David also says, "I have set the Lord continually before me."

That isn't about forcing a feeling or pretending everything is fine.

It's about remembering, moment by moment, that the God who loves you is near... always near... even in the ordinary, uneventful parts of your day.

A dog resting joyfully at your feet is a picture of that truth.

They aren't thrilled because something exciting is happening.

They aren't overwhelmed because life is perfect.

They're content because they're close to the one they love.

How different would our lives feel if we approached Jesus with that same heart?

What if our joy didn't rise and fall with circumstances?

What if our peace wasn't dependent on outcomes?

What if simply being near Jesus, sitting in His presence, welcoming His nearness, became our source of strength and delight?

We don't have to impress God to experience His presence.

We don't have to earn His attention.

We don't have to come with perfect words or spiritual

accomplishments.

He delights in being with us, and He invites us to delight in being with Him.

So often we chase joy in the wrong places.

We chase achievements.

We chase approval.

We chase comfort, distractions, new things, and quick fixes.

But none of those things bring lasting joy because none of them are constant.

Everything else shifts… but Jesus stays.

And when you learn to find joy in His presence, not His gifts, not His answers, not His timing, but Him, the world suddenly becomes a softer, steadier place. Worries shrink. Fears quiet. The noise of life dims. Your soul breathes deeper. Because joy has found its anchor not in circumstance but in relationship.

That's why dogs get it right in a way that we sometimes miss.

They're not celebrating what you've done, they're celebrating you.

And maybe, in the quiet places of your heart, God is inviting you to rediscover the joy of simply being with Him… just sitting near Him, breathing in His peace, letting His presence be enough.

Because closeness to Jesus is not just comforting, it is life-giving.

It is steadying.

It is healing.

It is joy in its purest form.

And when your heart learns to delight in Him, even the ordinary moments become holy ground.

Curl Up Close and Pray

Lord Jesus,

Thank You for the gift of Your presence. Thank You that You are not a distant God, not far away or unreachable, but near, closer than my thoughts, closer than my breath, closer than any circumstance or emotion I face. Teach my heart to find joy simply because You are here.

Sometimes I chase after joy in all the wrong places.

Sometimes I look for comfort in things that can't sustain me.

Sometimes I forget that what my heart truly longs for is not more activity, but more of You.

Draw me back into the quiet places where Your presence becomes my peace.

Help me rest at Your feet the way a dog rests at the feet of the one it loves, unhurried, unafraid, and content just to be near. Settle my spirit. Calm my busy thoughts. Let my heart breathe again in the warmth of Your nearness.

Lord, open my eyes to see You in the ordinary moments.

Help me recognize Your presence in the quiet, in the stillness, and even in the mundane routines of life. Let the simple awareness that You are with me fill my soul with a steady, unshakeable joy.

Thank You for being my refuge, my peace, my delight, and my joy.

Thank You that I never have to earn Your presence.

Thank You that You enjoy being near me, and that You invite me to enjoy being near You.

Teach me to delight in You, Lord.

Teach me to find fullness of joy in Your presence.

Teach me to rest at Your side with a heart that is warm, content, and deeply loved.

I love You, Jesus.
And I am thankful that You are always here.
Amen.

- 6 -

Muddy Paws and Mercy

Paws and Open Your Heart

If you've ever owned a dog, you know what it's like to hear that suspicious silence, the kind that makes you instinctively glance toward the back door. And sure enough, there they are, standing on the porch or padding through the hallway with paws caked in mud.

Not a little mud.

Not a polite dusting.

But the kind of mud that makes you wonder if they tunneled through a swamp, wrestled a puddle, and then rolled in it for good measure.

Their eyes widen when they see you.

Their tail gives a hesitant wag, the "I might be in trouble but I'm still happy to see you" wag.

And you stand there staring at them... at the mess dripping off their fur, at the pawprints already tracing a trail behind them, at the chaos they unknowingly carried straight into your clean house.

And in that moment, you have a choice.

You can scold.

You can yell.

You can get frustrated at the mess they made.

Or you can kneel down, lift their muddy paws, and help them get clean.

Because here's the truth every dog owner knows deep down:

A dog doesn't come to you clean, they come to you because you are the one who can make them clean.

They don't stay outside until they've fixed the mess on their own.

They come inside because they trust your hands more than their ability to fix it.

You watch their tail slowly wag as you wipe each paw.

You see the way they lean their head against you, relieved that your love is bigger than the trouble they stepped in.

And as you rinse away the mud, you notice something else, the mud never changed the way they loved you.

And it never changed the way you loved them either.

Because the mess wasn't the end of the relationship.

It was simply a moment for mercy.

Dogs never try to hide their muddy paws.

They don't run away ashamed.

They don't pretend they're clean.

They simply come, mess and all, right to the one who loves them.

And the way you kneel beside them, gently lifting each dirty paw, wiping away the grime, cleaning the fur between their toes… that moment is its own kind of grace. It's quiet, it's tender, and it whispers a truth you can feel deep down:

Love doesn't stop at the sight of a mess.

Love shows up to clean it.

If you've ever knelt over a muddy dog, hands wet, floor covered, yet heart soft… you've experienced something holy without even realizing it. You've felt the tug of mercy, mercy that doesn't wait for perfection, mercy that moves toward the mess, mercy that restores instead of rejects.

Because sometimes the ones we love come to us covered in mud.

And sometimes…

we are the ones standing on the porch with filthy paws, hoping love hasn't changed.

Scripture to Sink Your Teeth Into

Psalm 51:1–3, 7, 10 (AMP)

1 Have mercy on me, O God, according to Your lovingkindness;

According to the greatness of Your compassion blot out my transgressions.

2 Wash me thoroughly from my wickedness and guilt

And cleanse me from my sin.

3 For I am conscious of my transgressions [and I acknowledge them];

My sin is always before me.

7 Purify me with hyssop, and I will be clean;

Wash me, and I will be whiter than snow.

10 Create in me a clean heart, O God,

And renew a right and steadfast spirit within me.

Lesson To Chew On

Coming to Jesus With the Mess Still on Our Feet

There is something sacred hidden inside the simple act of wiping a dog's muddy paws, something that looks a whole lot like the heart of God. Because the truth is, we don't just track mud across our floors. We track it across our souls. We step into places we shouldn't have stepped. We wander through things that cling to us. We pick up stains, habits, attitudes, and choices that leave us feeling dirty, ashamed, and unsure whether we dare come back inside.

But here's the part we often forget:

Jesus doesn't ask us to clean ourselves up before we come to Him.

He asks us to come, so that He can clean us.

Dogs don't fix their mess on their own.

They don't stand outside waiting until the mud magically falls off.

They don't hide behind the bushes hoping you won't notice what they've done.

They simply come, mess and all, because they trust that the one who loves them will not reject them.

That is the picture David paints in Psalm 51.

"Wash me… Purify me… Create in me a clean heart."

David didn't pretend his mistakes weren't real.

He didn't try to explain away his sins.

He didn't hide behind excuses or distance.

He stepped onto God's porch with muddy feet and said,

"Lord, I've made a mess. I need Your mercy."

And God met him, not with anger, but with cleansing.

Not with rejection, but with restoration.

Not with shame, but with mercy.

Scripture says that God washes us "thoroughly," purifies us, renews us, and makes us whiter than snow. That's not the language of a God who is disgusted by our mess. That's the language of a God who kneels down, takes our trembling hands, and begins to clean us with love.

Every one of us has walked through mud.

Every one of us has brought something into God's presence that we wish we hadn't.

Every one of us knows what it feels like to stand on the doorstep wondering if we're still welcome.

But Jesus sees us standing there.

He sees the dirt.

He sees the stains.

He sees the trail behind us.

And He still opens the door.

Because His mercy is bigger than our mess.

His love is stronger than our failure.

His forgiveness is deeper than any stain we carry.

When a dog brings mud into the house, you don't stop loving them. You bend down and begin the work of cleaning because love chooses compassion over condemnation. In the same way, God doesn't turn us away. He doesn't shrink back from our dirt. He draws near. He cups our brokenness in His hands and says,

"Let Me make you clean again."

And here's the miracle of mercy:

The mess we fear the most becomes the moment His grace shines the brightest.

So come to Him, even with muddy paws.

Come even if you're embarrassed.

Come even if you feel unworthy.

Come even if you're afraid of what He will think.

Because the God who loves you isn't waiting to shame you,

He's waiting to wash you.

And in His hands, your mess becomes mercy.

Curl Up Close and Pray

Lord Jesus,

Thank You for loving me even when I make a mess of things. Thank You that Your mercy does not shrink back from my failures, my mistakes, or the muddy places my heart sometimes wanders into. Instead, You draw near to me with compassion, ready to cleanse, restore, and make me new.

I admit, Lord, that there are times I feel ashamed of the mess I bring into Your presence. Times when I hesitate at the door, unsure if I'm still welcome. Times when I try to hide my dirt or pretend it isn't as bad as it feels. But You already know every part of me, and still You invite me close.

So today I come, just as I am.

Not cleaned up.

Not perfect.

Not pretending.

But real, honest, and in need of Your mercy.

Wash me, Lord.

Cleanse my heart.

Wipe away the stains I cannot fix.

Restore the joy I've lost along the way.

Renew my spirit and make me whole again.

Thank You that Your love is stronger than my sin,

Your grace deeper than my failures,

and Your compassion greater than any mess I will ever bring to You.

Help me trust Your mercy, Jesus.

Help me come quickly when I've fallen.

Help me believe that nothing, nothing at all, can make You stop loving me.

Thank You for being the God who kneels down,

the God who cleans my muddy paws,

and the God who calls me His own even when I feel unworthy.

I love You, Lord.

And I'm grateful that Your mercy always meets me at the door.

Amen.

- 7 -
The Dog Who Waited

Paws and Open Your Heart

Some dogs have a way of waiting that feels almost human,
a patient, quiet kind of loyalty that doesn't rush, doesn't demand, and doesn't lose hope.

They simply wait.

Not anxiously.

Not frantically.

Not with fear in their eyes.

But with a calm certainty, as if something inside them knows the truth:

the one they love is coming back.

Maybe you've seen a dog like that,

the kind who sits by the front door, tail resting on the floor, eyes fixed on the knob even when the house is silent and the hours stretch long.

They don't whimper.

They don't pace.

They don't wander off to find a distraction.

They just wait.

There's a dignity in it, a kind of soulful stillness that makes you pause.

They don't know when you're coming home.

They don't know how long it will take.

They don't know whether you're five minutes away or five hours.

But they know you.

And that knowledge is enough.

Some dogs wait at the window, chin resting on the sill, ears tilting forward every time a car passes.

They perk up with each sound,

a door shutting, a voice outside, footsteps on the sidewalk,

hoping each one is the moment their waiting ends.

Others wait on the bed or the couch, lying in the spot where your scent is strongest, guarding it like a sacred memory.

They don't move much.

Their breathing stays slow, steady.

But their eyes never fully sleep.

They're always listening,

always ready to recognize the sound of your steps.

And then there are those dogs whose waiting becomes legendary,

stories about dogs who stayed by a bus stop, a train station, a front yard,

long after their owner was gone.

Dogs who didn't know why the world had changed.

Dogs who didn't understand what had happened.

They only knew one thing:

love stays.

Love waits.

Love remains faithful.

And so they waited with a loyalty that puts most of us to shame.

Not because they were commanded to,

but because deep affection shaped their nature.

Waiting, for a dog, isn't about time.

It's about relationship.

They wait because their heart is tied to yours.

They wait because your return is worth it.

They wait because love, real love, holds on.

And when the moment finally comes,

when they hear your voice,

when the key rattles,
when you open the door,
their entire body erupts in joy.
Not once do they say,
"Why did you take so long?"
Not once do they punish you by staying away.
Not once do they hold back their happiness.
The waiting melts instantly into celebration.
Because for them, love has only one response to reunion:
joy without hesitation.
And isn't it beautiful,
how a creature who cannot speak with words
can teach us something profound with the way they wait?
If you've ever seen a dog wait faithfully,
day after day,
moment after moment,
you've witnessed a glimpse of something holy:
A love that waits…
and a heart that refuses to give up on the one it adores.

Scripture to Sink Your Teeth Into

Isaiah 40:28–31 (AMP)
28 Do you not know? Have you not heard?
The everlasting God, the Lord, the Creator of the ends of the earth does not become tired or grow weary;
There is no searching of His understanding.
29 He gives strength to the weary,
And to him who has no might He increases power.
30 Even youths grow weary and tired,
And vigorous young men stumble badly,
31 But those who wait for the Lord [who expect, look for, and

hope in Him]

Will gain new strength and renew their power;

They will lift up their wings [and rise up close to God] like eagles,

They will run and not become weary,

They will walk and not grow tired.

Lesson To Chew On

Learning to Wait With Loyal Love and Steady Hope

Waiting is one of the most stretching, soul-shaping experiences of the Christian life. Not because waiting is slow, but because waiting is revealing. It uncovers what we trust, what we fear, what we love, and what we believe about God's heart toward us. And sometimes, the quiet faithfulness of a dog who waits speaks louder than the hurried pace of our own hearts.

A dog doesn't wait because it has a detailed plan or timeline.

It waits because it trusts the one it loves.

It waits with steady eyes, quiet hope, and unwavering loyalty.

It waits because love has taught it something time cannot shake:

"They may be gone for a moment, but they are coming back."

Isaiah 40 says that those who wait for the Lord,

those who expect Him, look for Him, hope in Him,

gain new strength.

Not borrowed strength.

Not leftover strength.

New strength.

Strength born in the waiting, not after it.

Waiting for God does not weaken you,

it renews you.

It teaches your heart to lean, not on answers,

but on the One who holds the answers.

But let's be honest…

waiting doesn't feel like renewal.

Waiting often feels like uncertainty.

Waiting can feel like silence.

Waiting can feel like standing at a window with a heart that wonders,

"Lord… will You really come through?"

Yet Scripture doesn't simply tell us to wait,

it tells us how to wait.

To wait with expectation.

To wait with hope.

To wait believing He is faithful.

To wait because we know His character,

not because we understand His timing.

A dog never doubts your return simply because time passes.

They don't assume delay means you're gone forever.

They don't believe silence means abandonment.

They wait with steady affection because their heart knows something truer than the passing hours:

Your love will bring you back.

We, on the other hand, often treat God differently.

We give Him deadlines.

We get discouraged when nothing changes.

We wonder if He heard our prayer, or if we prayed wrong, or if something's broken.

We mistake delay for indifference, silence for distance, and waiting for abandonment.

But Isaiah reminds us:

God does not grow weary.

God does not forget.

God does not fail.

God does not disappear.

He is always working, always moving, always preparing,

even when we don't see movement yet.

When you learn to wait like the dog who waits for its beloved,

with loyalty, love, and unwavering confidence,
you discover a beautiful truth:
Waiting is not inactivity.
Waiting is trust in motion.
And the moment God steps into the situation you've been praying about,
just like the dog who erupts with joy at the sound of your return,
your weary heart will find its strength renewed, its hope revived, and its faith lifted like wings on the wind.
Because waiting on God is never wasted.
Never lost.
Never ignored.
Never overlooked.
The God who calls you to wait
is the God who always, always, always
comes through in perfect time.

Curl Up Close and Pray

Lord Jesus,
Thank You for being a God who is always faithful, always present, and always worth waiting for. You know how easily my heart grows impatient, how quickly I become discouraged, and how often I struggle to trust what I cannot see. But You, Lord, never grow weary, never forget me, and never fail to come through in perfect time.
Teach me to wait the way a loyal dog waits,
not with fear or anxiety,
but with quiet confidence and steady hope.
Help me believe that even when nothing seems to be changing,
You are still working.

You are still moving.
You are still writing the story in ways I cannot yet see.
When waiting feels long, give me strength.
When silence feels heavy, give me peace.
When doubt whispers, give me truth.
When my hope feels tired, renew it as only You can.
Lord, help me fix my eyes on You not on the timing,
not on the circumstances,
not on the what-ifs,
but on Your heart,
the heart of a Shepherd who never abandons His own.
Thank You for the promise that those who wait for You
will rise up in strength,
will walk and not faint,
will run and not grow weary.
Help me trust that promise, even in the stillness.
And when the moment comes,
when You step into the situation I've been praying about,
when You bring clarity, healing, provision, or direction,
let my heart respond with joy,
with gratitude,
with the same unfiltered celebration that a dog shows when
the one they love returns.
Thank You for being worth the wait.
Thank You for never letting go.
And thank You for teaching my heart to wait with hope.
I love You, Jesus.
Amen.

- 8 -

When the Master Speaks

Paws and Open Your Heart

There is a moment every dog owner treasures,
a moment when the dog hears your voice and everything in them shifts.

They can be running full-speed across the yard, nose buried in the grass, lost in a world of smells and distractions…
but then you speak.

And suddenly, they stop.

Their ears lift.

Their head turns.

Their body freezes in that unmistakable pose of recognition.

It's as if the entire world goes silent for one sacred second, and the only sound that matters is the voice they trust most.

Dogs don't respond that way to every voice.

They don't perk up at the neighbor's shout.

They don't turn around when a stranger calls.

They don't change direction at just any noise.

But your voice?

The one that feeds them, comforts them, trains them, and loves them?

They know that voice.

They follow that voice.

They respond to that voice, even before they understand what you're asking.

And sometimes, your voice is all it takes to settle their heart.

Think about the times a dog gets startled by thunder, fireworks, or an unfamiliar sound.

Their body trembles, their eyes widen, their breath quickens...
but then you speak softly,
and something inside them melts.
Your voice becomes their shelter.
Your words calm the storm inside them.
Your presence steadies the fear they don't know how to explain.
Other times, your voice becomes their guide.
A gentle "Come here."
A firm "Leave it."
A reassuring "It's okay."
A joyful "Good boy!"
You don't even need to speak loudly,
sometimes just the tone of your voice is enough for them to know what to do.
And in moments of distraction, when a dog is about to wander too far or chase something dangerous, your voice becomes the lifeline that pulls them back to safety.
Even dogs who struggle to obey...
even dogs who are stubborn or easily distracted...
even dogs who get caught up in the excitement of the moment...
still respond when the master speaks.
They may hesitate.
They may pause.
They may look back and weigh their options.
But they know your voice,
and deep down, they want to follow it.
Because voice recognition, for a dog, isn't about intellect.
It's about relationship.
Your voice is familiar.
Your voice is safe.
Your voice means love.
Your voice means home.

And if you've ever watched a dog respond instantly to just the sound of your words, you've seen something profoundly beautiful,

a creature whose heart and ears have been trained by love to recognize the one who cares for them most.

A dog's whole world can shift with a single word from its master.

And maybe…

just maybe…

there's a truth there for our souls too.

Scripture to Sink Your Teeth Into

John 10:3–5, 14, 27 (AMP)

3 The doorkeeper opens [the gate] for this man, and the sheep hear his voice and pay attention to it. And knowing that they listen, he calls his own sheep by name and leads them out.

4 When he has brought all his own sheep outside, he walks on ahead of them, and the sheep follow him because they know his voice and recognize his call.

5 They will never follow a stranger, but will run away from him because they do not know the voice of strangers.

14 I am the Good Shepherd, and I know [without any doubt] those who are My own and My own know Me [and have a deep, personal relationship with Me],

27 The sheep that are My own hear My voice and listen to Me; I know them, and they follow Me.

Lesson To Chew On

Recognizing the Voice That Leads Us Home

There is something quietly profound about the way a dog knows its master's voice. Not because someone taught them a formula or gave them a list of reasons, but because they have lived close enough, long enough, to recognize the sound of love. Their ears have been shaped by the relationship. Their heart is tuned by familiarity.

And that's exactly what Jesus speaks about in John 10.

He doesn't say,

"My sheep follow Me because they understand everything I say."

He doesn't say,

"My sheep follow Me because every command makes sense."

He says:

"My sheep hear My voice… and they follow Me."

Hearing comes before understanding.

Recognition comes before obedience.

Relationship comes before instruction.

A dog doesn't pause in the backyard to analyze the meaning of your words.

They don't break down your tone grammatically.

They don't weigh every command against their feelings.

They simply know you,

and because they know you, they follow.

If only our hearts learned to trust Jesus with that same simplicity.

We often overcomplicate the voice of God.

We second-guess it.

We talk ourselves out of it.

We assume we must be mistaken, or unworthy, or imagining

things.

We wait for a lightning bolt when all along, Jesus is speaking in the steady, familiar tone of love.

And while a dog responds to your voice instantly, we humans tend to hesitate.

We hear Jesus whisper "Come," and we stall.

We sense Him saying "Let go," and we cling tighter.

We feel Him guiding us toward a step of obedience, and fear convinces us to freeze.

But Scripture says His sheep not only hear His voice,
they recognize it.

Recognition doesn't come from religious performance,
it comes from relationship.

It comes from leaning in.

It comes from quiet moments with Him.

It comes from listening even when we don't feel spiritual.

It comes from reading His Word until His tone becomes familiar.

It comes from prayer, not fancy, polished prayer, but honest prayer,
the kind where you talk to Him like He's really there... because He is.

A dog knows its master's voice because it hears that voice every day.

Our hearts grow to recognize Jesus' voice the same way,
through daily nearness, daily presence, daily listening.

And here's the beauty of it:
Jesus doesn't speak to confuse you.

He speaks to lead you.

He speaks to protect you.

He speaks to guide you back when you wander too far.

He speaks to calm your fears when the world feels loud and frightening.

He speaks because He knows your name,
and He calls you with the gentleness of a Shepherd who deeply loves His sheep.

A dog doesn't follow every voice.

They follow the voice that has fed them, comforted them, guided them, and loved them.

Likewise, Jesus wants us to respond to His voice above all others,

the voice that offers truth, peace, safety, purpose, correction, and belonging.

And when you begin to recognize that voice…

when you learn to pause, listen, and respond…

your whole world shifts.

Your fears quiet.

Your direction becomes clearer.

Your obedience becomes easier.

Your heart grows steadier.

Because the voice you're following

is the voice that leads you home.

Curl Up Close and Pray

Lord Jesus,

Thank You for being the Shepherd who speaks to His sheep with love, patience, and gentleness. Thank You that You do not shout over the noise of the world, but call me by name, inviting me to trust You, follow You, and walk close to You.

Teach my heart to recognize Your voice.

Teach my spirit to lean in when You speak.

Teach my ears to listen, not to fear, not to doubt, not to the noise around me, but to You.

So many voices compete for my attention.

Voices of worry, voices of pressure, voices of temptation, voices of discouragement.

But Your voice, Lord, is the one that brings peace.

Your voice brings truth.
Your voice brings clarity.
Your voice brings life.
Help me become familiar with the sound of Your heart.
Help me learn the tone of Your love.
Help me sense Your guidance even in quiet whispers.
Let Your Word shape the way I hear You,
and let time spent with You tune my heart like an instrument,
so that when You speak, I know it's You.
Lord, when You call me, help me come quickly.
When You warn me, help me turn back.
When You comfort me, help me rest in Your arms.
When You guide me, help me follow without fear.
Thank You that I am not a stranger to You.
Thank You that You know me, deeply, personally, completely.
And thank You that when You speak, it is always for my good.
Let Your voice be the anchor of my life.
Let Your words shape my steps.
Let Your presence be my home.
I love You, Jesus.
Help me walk close enough to hear You clearly.
Amen.

- 9 -

Walking the Same Path

Paws and Open Your Heart

One of the sweetest things about a dog is how deeply they love to walk beside you.

It doesn't matter where you're headed,

down a quiet road, through a forest trail, around the block, or just from room to room,

if you're going, they want to go too.

There's something almost sacred in the way a dog falls into step with the one they love.

They don't need to understand the plan.

They don't ask where you're going or how long it will take.

They're not worried about the destination.

All they care about is the simple, beautiful truth:

You're walking, and they want to walk with you.

Some dogs stay so close their fur brushes your leg with every step, matching your pace without thinking.

Others run a little ahead, excited, ears bouncing, glancing back every few seconds to make sure you're still coming.

Some walk behind you, content to follow your lead, taking in the world but always keeping you in their sights.

But wherever they are positioned, one thing never changes:

their path is shaped by yours.

A dog doesn't carve its own trail when you are near.

They don't wander off in a hundred directions when you're walking.

Your steps become their steps.

Your pace becomes their pace.

Your direction becomes their direction.

And even when distractions pull at their attention,

a squirrel darting across the yard,

a scent drifting through the air,

a noise off in the distance,

they always come back to your side.

Because the walk isn't about exploring the world,

it's about being with you.

There's a comfort in it that runs deeper than we realize.

A dog walking at your side isn't simply exercising,

they are bonding.

They are trusting.

They are choosing you over every distraction around them.

And if you've ever walked a trail or a sidewalk or even a familiar hallway with a dog at your side, you know the quiet beauty of that companionship,

the soft rhythm of paws on the ground,

the gentle jingle of a collar,

the way their presence keeps you company without a single word spoken.

Sometimes they look up at you mid-walk, eyes shining with that silent expression that says,

"I love being wherever you are."

They're not interested in arriving quickly.

They're not frustrated by how long the journey takes.

They're not rushing ahead because they want to finish early.

They're just enjoying the walk,

because the walk is time spent with you.

And that's the part that stirs the heart:

you don't have to be doing anything extraordinary.

You don't have to speak profound words.

You don't have to impress them.

You just have to be there.

Your presence is the gift.

Your companionship is enough.

Your steps are the rhythm that guides their own.

And maybe that's why walking with a dog feels sacred,

because in their simple, loyal devotion, you catch a glimpse of what it means to walk the same path with someone you trust.

Scripture to Sink Your Teeth Into

Psalm 25:4–5, 9–10 (AMP)
4 Let me know Your ways, O Lord;

Teach me Your paths.
5 Guide me in Your truth and teach me,
For You are the God of my salvation;
For You [and only You] I wait [expectantly] all the day long.
9 He leads the humble in justice,
And He teaches the humble His way.
10 All the paths of the Lord are lovingkindness and goodness
and truth and faithfulness
To those who keep His covenant and His testimonies.

Lesson To Chew On

Letting Your Steps Fall in Rhythm With Jesus

There is something deeply moving about the way a dog chooses to walk beside the one it loves. They don't walk with you because they have to. They don't walk with you because they're afraid of getting lost. And they don't walk with you because they understand every turn you're about to make. They walk with you because their joy is found in your nearness.

What a picture of the relationship God desires with us.

In Psalm 25, David prays, "Teach me Your paths… Guide me in Your truth… Lead me."

It's the language of someone who doesn't want to walk ahead of God or lag behind Him, but someone who desires to walk with Him, step by step, pace by pace, heart by heart.

Just like a dog matches its stride to yours, Scripture invites us to match our steps with Jesus.

But walking with God isn't always as effortless for us as it is for a dog.

Distractions tug at us.

Worries pull us sideways.

Temptations lure us off the trail.

Old habits whisper their familiar directions.

And sometimes we find ourselves wandering without even realizing how far we've drifted.

Yet when a dog wanders too far, you call them back, gently but firmly, and they return because they trust your voice.

God does the same with us.

He leads the humble.

He teaches the willing.

He guides the open-hearted.

He invites us back to the path again and again because His desire is not for perfection, but companionship.

And that is the heart of this devotion:

God doesn't just want you to believe in Him,

He wants you to walk with Him.

A walk is not hurried.

A walk is not frantic.

A walk is not a sprint toward a finish line.

A walk is relational.

It's steady.

It's rhythmic.

It's shared.

Some days you will feel strong and energetic, eager to keep pace.

Other days you will feel tired, distracted, or discouraged. But the beauty is this:

Jesus never changes His pace to leave you behind.

He changes His pace to stay beside you.

Just as a dog slows down when you slow down, pauses when you pause, and waits when you need a moment, Jesus does the same with you.

He walks with you at the pace your soul can handle.

He doesn't rush your healing.

He doesn't force your growth.

He doesn't drag you forward.

He simply stays close, guiding, nudging, steadying, encouraging.

And when you stumble, He doesn't scold you for slowing the journey.

He helps you back up and keeps walking with you.

When David says, "All the paths of the Lord are lovingkindness and goodness," he is reminding us that God's way is not harsh or punishing, it's shaped by love. Every path God leads you down is filled with purpose, and every step you take with Him draws your heart closer to His.

Walking the same path with Jesus means this:

You don't walk alone.

You don't walk without purpose.

You don't walk without guidance.

You don't walk without love marking the ground beneath your feet.

It means choosing presence over self-direction, trust over independence, and companionship over control.

The dog walking at your side isn't questioning the destination, they're enjoying the journey because they're with the one they love.

And that's the kind of simple, steady, faithful companionship God invites you into each day.

Not just believing in Him…

but walking with Him.

Curl Up Close and Pray

Lord Jesus,

Thank You for inviting me to walk with You, not behind You in fear, not ahead of You in pride, but beside You in trust. Thank You that Your desire is not just to lead me, but to be with me every step of the journey.

Teach my heart to find joy in simply being close to You.

Teach my soul to match its pace to Yours.

Teach me to listen for Your guidance, to lean into Your presence, and to follow Your steps with confidence and peace.

There are days, Lord, when distractions pull me off the path.

There are moments when worries cause me to wander, and times when discouragement slows my feet.

But You never leave me behind.

You stay near, gently drawing me back, reminding me that Your path is always paved with love, goodness, and truth.

Help me walk humbly with You,

not rushing ahead,

not lagging behind,

but staying close enough to hear Your voice

and steady enough to follow where You lead.

Lord, when I don't know which way to go,

be my Guide.

When I grow weary,

be my Strength.

When I feel lost,

be my Shepherd.

Let my life be a long walk with You,

step by step,

day by day,

moment by moment,

a journey marked not by perfection, but by companionship.

Thank You that Your presence turns every path,

even the difficult ones,

into a place where I can find peace.

I love walking with You, Lord.

Help me treasure the journey as much as the destination.

Amen.

- 10 -
The Empty Bowl

Paws and Open Your Heart

Dog owners know there is a certain look,
a look that appears the moment a dog discovers their food bowl is empty.

Sometimes they sit beside it, staring down into the smooth, clean bottom like they're contemplating the great mysteries of the universe.

Sometimes they nudge it gently with their nose, hoping maybe, just maybe, food might magically appear if they try hard enough.

Sometimes they sit back on their haunches and give you that long, soulful stare, the kind that says,

"Human… something has gone terribly wrong."

And if the bowl stays empty long enough, you might hear a quiet whine,

or the gentle scrape of a paw on the floor,

or the unmistakable sound of metal tapping as they try to get your attention.

A dog doesn't hide its hunger.

They don't pretend everything is fine.

They don't try to fill the emptiness with something else.

They simply bring their need to the one they trust.

Because to a dog, an empty bowl is not a crisis,

it's a message.

A message that says:

"I need what only you can give."

"I trust you to notice."

"I know you will take care of me."

And what's beautiful is how confident they are in your provision.

They don't panic.

They don't assume you've forgotten them forever.

They don't conclude that you no longer care.

They simply wait, watching with those steady, hopeful eyes, believing that the one who has fed them every day of their life will feed them again today.

Sometimes their hunger makes them more affectionate, they lean against you, follow you from room to room, or sit at your feet with the quiet expectation of one who knows they are loved, they are seen, they are cared for.

And when you finally fill the bowl, the relief that washes over them is pure joy.

Not just because of the food, but because their trust was not misplaced.

A dog never doubts its owner's ability to provide.

A dog never questions whether it will be fed tomorrow.

A dog never carries anxiety about its next meal.

Its heart is anchored in the daily faithfulness it has already experienced.

And here's something even more beautiful: a dog doesn't just trust you for physical food.

They trust you for comfort, for presence, for affection, for companionship.

Their whole life revolves around the simple truth that you are the one who provides what they need.

An empty bowl doesn't frighten them,

because they know it won't stay empty for long.

And if you've ever knelt beside a waiting dog,

pouring food into that bowl and watching their tail thump in relief,

you've felt the sweetness of meeting a need

in someone who completely trusts your heart.

It's a glimpse into a deeper truth,

a truth about daily dependence,

daily hunger,

and daily trust.

Scripture to Sink Your Teeth Into

Matthew 6:25–26, 31–33 (AMP)

25 "Therefore I tell you, stop being worried or anxious (perpetually uneasy, distracted) about your life…

26 Look at the birds of the air; they neither sow [seed] nor reap [the harvest] nor gather [the crops] into barns, and yet your heavenly Father keeps feeding them. Are you not worth much more than they?"

31 "Therefore do not worry or be anxious, saying, 'What are we going to eat?' or 'What are we going to drink?' or 'What are we going to wear?'"

32 "…for your heavenly Father knows that you need them."

33 "But first and most importantly seek (aim at, strive after) His kingdom and His righteousness [His way of doing and being right, the attitude and character of God], and all these things will be given to you also."

Lesson To Chew On

Trusting God When Your Bowl Feels Empty

There is something tender and quietly profound in the way a dog responds to an empty bowl. They do not panic. They do not spiral into fear. They do not question your love or doubt your care. They simply look to you, the one who has always provided, and wait with gentle expectation.

They know the bowl won't stay empty forever.

They know help is coming.

They know who their provider is.

And in their simple trust, they reveal something our hearts often struggle to live out.

Because when our "bowl" feels empty,

when money feels tight,

or strength feels low,

or hope feels thin,

or clarity feels missing,

or our emotional reserves feel drained,

we tend to worry, fear, and assume the worst.

We stare at the emptiness as if it is permanent.

We question God's timing.

We wonder whether He sees us, whether He knows our need, whether He is still working.

But Jesus gently reminds us in Matthew 6 that our Father already knows what we need.

He sees the emptiness before we even pray.

He is not surprised by our hunger.

He is not unaware of our situation.

He is not indifferent to our needs.

And just like the dog who sits by the empty bowl with quiet confidence,

Jesus invites us to rest in the same kind of trust.
Not frantic worry.
Not anxious striving.
Not fear-driven conclusions.
Just trust.
Because emptiness is often where faith begins to grow.
The bird does not panic about its next meal.
The flower does not worry about its clothing.
And the dog does not doubt the one who fills the bowl.
Jesus uses simple, everyday things to teach a profound truth:
You are more valuable than any creature He has ever made,
and He takes care of them daily.
How much more will He take care of you?
The empty bowl moments in life are not evidence of God's absence,
they are invitations to trust His presence.
They are reminders that:
- God's timing is perfect.
- God's provision is faithful.
- God's awareness is constant.
- God's love is never uncertain.
We are the ones who grow anxious.
We are the ones who overthink.
We are the ones who assume the worst.
But God remains steady, loving, attentive, and generous.
And here's the beautiful truth:
Your bowl will not stay empty.
Not emotionally,
not spiritually,
not physically,
not in any area where you place your trust in Him.
He knows what you need.
He sees your hunger.
He hears your quiet cries.
He understands the longing you cannot put into words.
And He is already working to provide,

maybe not in the way you expect,
maybe not in the timing you prefer,
but always in the way that is best.
So instead of fearing the emptiness,
do what the dog does:
Bring your need to the One who can fill it.
Sit near Him.
Wait with expectancy.
Trust His heart, even if you don't yet see His hand.
Because the God who has cared for you all your life
is not about to stop now.

Curl Up Close and Pray

Lord Jesus,

Thank You for being the One who sees every empty place in my life, every need, every longing, every fear, every hunger I carry inside. Thank You that nothing I face is hidden from You, and nothing I lack is overlooked by You.

Teach my heart to trust You the way a loyal dog trusts the one who fills its bowl,

with confidence,

with peace,

with quiet expectation,

and without fear.

There are moments, Lord, when my "bowl" feels painfully empty.

Times when my strength runs low,

when my joy feels thin,

when my resources seem stretched,

when my hope wavers.

In those moments, help me not to panic or assume the worst,

but to stay near You,
waiting, trusting, believing that You will provide.
You have never failed me.
You have never forgotten me.
You have never abandoned me in my need.
So help me rest in Your faithfulness today.
Fill what is empty in me, Lord.
Pour peace where anxiety has settled.
Pour strength where weakness has grown.
Pour hope where discouragement whispers.
Pour provision where resources are lacking.
Open Your hand, as Your Word promises,
and satisfy my need in Your perfect way and timing.
And Lord, while I wait,
help me seek You first,
not the answers,
not the solutions,
not the outcomes,
but You.
Because You are the true bread that satisfies,
the living water that fills my soul,
the Provider whose love never fails.
Thank You for being good.
Thank You for being faithful.
Thank You for caring for me more deeply than I can understand.
I trust You, Jesus.
My bowl is in Your hands.
Amen.

- 11 -
A Dog's Faithfulness

Paws and Open Your Heart

There is a faithfulness in a dog that feels almost ancient, as if it was woven into them long before you ever knew their name. Some dogs express it loudly, following you from room to room, tapping their paws like a soft drumbeat behind you, always settling exactly where you settle as if some invisible thread connects their heart to your steps. Others express it quietly, a soft presence resting at your feet, a warm body curled beside your chair, a pair of gentle eyes watching your face as if your expression alone tells them everything they need to know about the moment. And then there are the dogs whose faithfulness shows up in the small, ordinary rhythms that many people overlook: the dog who patiently waits outside the bathroom door, the one who stands guard during your nap, the one who lifts its head at every sound simply because you walked into the room.

Faithfulness in a dog isn't dramatic; it's steady. It doesn't demand attention, applause, or thanks. It shows up every morning and every night. It walks beside you when you're smiling. It leans against you when you're sad. It sits close when you feel lonely and somehow understands that you don't need words, you just need presence. It is faithfulness shaped not by perfection but by love, not by obligation but by deep affection for the one they consider home.

There's something remarkable about how quickly a dog's

loyalty becomes woven into the fabric of your life. You begin to expect their footsteps behind you, that soft sigh as they settle at your side, the way they greet you with the same gladness no matter how long you were gone, five minutes or five hours, it doesn't matter. Their joy is always full, always sincere, always new. They are not calculating whether you deserve it that day. They are not weighing whether you were kind enough, patient enough, or generous enough. Their love is not earned by performance, it is anchored in relationship. In their mind, you belong to them, and they belong to you, and that belonging shapes everything.

Sometimes you see their faithfulness most clearly in the quiet hours of the night. A storm shakes the windows, and they move closer. You shift in bed, and they lift their head as if checking on you. You get up for a moment, and they follow, tail low and eyes soft, not out of fear but out of devotion. They simply want to be where you are. Their nearness is their gift. Their presence is their promise. And it's humbling to realize that they do all of this without ever saying a single word.

There is a beauty in that kind of faithfulness, a purity, a simplicity, a depth that asks nothing in return except the chance to stay near you. A dog doesn't wonder whether you'll still love them tomorrow. They trust your love the way they trust the sunrise. They don't fear abandonment with every mistake. They don't hide from you when they're unsure. They come to you because their heart already knows where safety lives. And in their ordinary, everyday devotion, they reveal a truth about love that many of us forget: love is not proven in grand gestures. It is proven in steady presence.

If you have ever looked into the eyes of a dog who sits faithfully beside you, waiting, watching, simply being with you, you know how deeply their constancy settles into your soul. For as long as they live, they give you a picture of something strong, something loyal, something steadfast. They show you what it means to stay. And in their gentle, unwavering companionship, they offer a glimpse of a faithfulness that points to something greater, something divine, something that reflects the heart of the One who has never once left your side.

Scripture to Sink Your Teeth Into

Lamentations 3:22–23 (AMP)
22 It is because of the Lord's loving kindnesses that we are not consumed, because His tender compassions never fail.
23 They are new every morning; great and beyond measure is Your faithfulness.

Lesson To Chew On

Faithfulness is a rare and precious thing in this world. People promise it easily but often struggle to live it out. Circumstances shift, emotions change, seasons come and go, and even the best intentions can falter under pressure. But a dog, in its simple and honest way, offers a picture of faithfulness that doesn't waver. They don't base their devotion on how well life is going. They don't measure their loyalty by whether things are convenient. They don't step back from you when life becomes messy, difficult, or complicated. They remain. And in that quiet, steadfast presence, they teach us something profound about the heart of God.

Lamentations tells us that God's faithfulness is "new every morning." Not recycled. Not drained. Not used up. Fresh. Renewed. Constant. That means that no matter what happened yesterday, the doubts you carried, the mistakes you made, the moments that felt too heavy to hold, God's faithfulness meets you again today just as strong as ever. He doesn't pull back. He doesn't reconsider. He doesn't decide you've crossed a line. His faithfulness does not depend on your performance but on His character. And His character never changes.

A dog's faithfulness mirrors that truth in miniature. They don't require explanations when you're tired, or withdrawn, or not at your best. They don't keep records of how often you've been frustrated or busy or distracted. They simply stay, believing that staying is part of love. In the same way, God stays, not because you always get it right, but because He promised He would. His faithfulness is not fragile. It is not conditional. It is not something that can be broken by one bad day. He is faithful because faithfulness is who He is.

Sometimes, when life becomes overwhelming, we look at our circumstance and wonder whether God has stepped back. We question His timing. We question His presence. We question His plan. But if we could see what is happening beneath the surface, we would discover that even when nothing feels stable, God is holding us with a faithfulness far stronger than anything we feel. We see delay; He sees development. We see silence; He sees preparation. We see confusion; He sees the path ahead with clarity. And in every moment, whether we recognize it or not, He is faithful.

A dog's daily devotion, its eagerness to be near, its joy at your return, its quiet companionship, reminds us that relationship is not maintained by occasional bursts of affection but by steady nearness. God doesn't ask you to be perfect; He asks you to stay close. His faithfulness doesn't fade when you struggle; it deepens. His compassion isn't discouraged by your weakness; it meets you there. And His devotion to you isn't diminished when you wander; it patiently guides you back to His side.

If you have ever been comforted by the presence of a loyal dog, you've tasted a small, earthly reflection of a holy truth: you are loved with a faithfulness stronger than circumstance, deeper than failure, and more constant than the rising sun. God's faithfulness doesn't simply follow you, it upholds you. It surrounds you. It carries you. And when you begin to trust that truth, your heart learns to rest in a love that will never leave, never falter, never change.

Curl Up Close and Pray

Lord Jesus,

thank You for the gift of faithfulness, both in the companions who walk beside us on earth and in the steadfast love that flows from Your heart. Help me recognize the ways You remain close to me even when I am distracted, discouraged, or unsure. Teach me to trust Your steady presence the way a loyal dog trusts the one they love. Renew my heart each morning with the reminder that Your mercies are fresh, Your compassion unfailing, and Your faithfulness unshakable. Help me walk in the confidence that I am never alone, never forgotten, and never abandoned. Thank You for being the constant presence my soul needs.

Amen.

- 12 -
Running to the Shepherd

Paws and Open Your Heart

There is a certain kind of run a dog makes that is different from every other run they have. It is not the joyful, bouncing sprint across the yard when they're chasing a ball or exploring a smell. It is not the proud, prancing run they make when carrying a stick twice their size. It is not the energetic "zoomies" that leave you laughing as they race in circles, overflowing with life. No, this run is something entirely different. It is the run that happens when fear steps into the room. A sound cracks across the sky, a sudden noise echoes down the hallway, or something unfamiliar rattles the world around them, and in one instant you see it, the flinch, the tremble, the pause that lasts only a heartbeat before their decision is made. And then they run. But what is beautiful, what is deeply tender, is that they do not run aimlessly. They run to you.

Fear never sends them hiding under a bed or escaping into another room the way it might for some animals. Instead, their paws hurry toward your presence, their body drawn toward the one place in the entire world where safety feels real. You are the shelter they trust more than any shadow, sound, or storm. They can be shaking, wide-eyed, unsure of what is happening, but their fear does not push them away from you, it pushes them closer. They press their trembling body against your legs, crawl into your lap, or tuck themselves under your arm as if wrapping their world inside yours will settle everything back into place. They do not ask whether you want them close. They do not worry about whether they are being too needy or dramatic. They don't stop to wonder whether you are disappointed in their fear. They simply run because instinct tells them what experience has already proven: when they reach you, they are safe.

And there is something remarkable about how complete their trust becomes in that moment. You don't have to fix the storm outside. You don't have to silence the noise. You don't have to make everything calm and perfect. Your presence alone changes them. Their breathing slows. Their muscles loosen. Their tail, tucked tight only moments before, begins to relax. Their eyes soften as if the fear inside of them is melting away simply because they reached the one they believe can handle the world better than they can. It is a humbling thing to be the place where a creature finds refuge. You feel it in the way they lean heavily against you, in the way they look up with that mixture of vulnerability and complete dependence, in the way they settle into your presence as though your nearness is more powerful than the storm that frightened them.

Some dogs do this every time a thunderstorm rolls in. Others do it when fireworks crack the sky or when the house makes a sound they do not recognize. Some run to you whenever someone new steps onto the property or when a door slams unexpectedly. And sometimes, it isn't fear of noise at all, sometimes it is the fear of loneliness, the fear of uncertainty, the fear of sensing that something in the house feels different or unsettled. But whatever the reason, their instinct remains the same. They run to the one they trust. They run to the one who has cared for them, fed them, protected them, loved them, and stayed with them. They run to their shepherd.

And if you've ever had a dog run to you like that, full of fear, full of trembling, full of trust, you know how powerful that moment feels. You see their need, and all you want to do is gather them close, hold them still, and whisper that everything will be alright. And somewhere inside that moment is a tender truth that reaches deep into the soul: the one who runs to the shepherd is never turned away.

Scripture to Sink Your Teeth Into

Psalm 34:4 (AMP)
"I sought the Lord [on the authority of His word], and He answered me, and delivered me from all my fears."

Lesson To Chew On

There is something sacred hidden inside the simple act of a dog running to the one they trust when fear breaks into their world. They don't hesitate. They don't analyze. They don't debate whether they should be stronger or braver or more composed. They don't run away in shame because they're afraid. They run straight to the one they love. And in that moment, we are given a glimpse into the kind of relationship God longs to have with us, one where fear doesn't push us away from Him but pulls us toward Him.

Fear has a way of revealing what we truly believe. It uncovers where we place our security, where we anchor our hope, and where we run when life feels overwhelming. Some people run inward, trying to gather enough strength to stand firm on their own. Some run outward, looking for distraction or escape. Some run nowhere at all, paralyzed by the weight of what they cannot control. But Scripture paints a different picture, one where fear becomes an invitation rather than an enemy. "I sought the Lord," David wrote, "and He delivered me from all my fears." Notice he didn't say God delivered him from the source of the fear first. He delivered him from the fear itself. The storm didn't have to stop before peace arrived. The danger didn't have to disappear before confidence returned. The circumstances didn't have to change before his heart did. It was God's presence, His nearness, that brought deliverance.

When a dog runs to you trembling, you don't scold them for their fear. You don't tell them to be tougher or braver. You don't demand that they stop shaking before they come near. You simply gather them in, hold them close, and let them rest in the safety of your presence. That is the heart of the Shepherd toward His children. God never said, "Do not fear because you are strong." He said, "Do not fear, for I am with you." Fear loses its power not because we become confident in ourselves, but because we become anchored in Him.

Many believers secretly struggle with the idea that they must approach God with strength, composure, and emotional stability. They think coming to Him fearful is somehow a failure of faith. But faith is not measured by the absence of fear, it is measured by where we run when fear comes. A dog running to its owner during a storm is not displaying weakness; it is displaying trust. In the same way, running to Jesus in times of fear is not immaturity, it is intimacy. It is the heart saying, "I cannot handle this alone, but I know who can."

And when we run to Him, God does what you do when a trembling dog presses itself into your arms: He meets us with gentleness. He meets us with compassion. He meets us with calm strength. He doesn't demand explanations for our fear. He doesn't push us away because we are shaking. He doesn't shame us for feeling overwhelmed. He welcomes us. He holds us. He steadies us. And slowly, the fear inside begins to melt, not because the storm outside has vanished, but because the Shepherd is near.

A dog running to its master is a living parable of what the Christian life was meant to look like, fear becomes a doorway to deeper dependence, storms become opportunities for nearness, and every trembling moment becomes a chance to discover the strength of the One who loves us. We learn that God is not put off by our fear; He invites us to bring it to Him. We learn that the safest place to be in any storm is not away from Him, but pressed close to His side. And we learn that running to the Shepherd is not something to outgrow, but something to practice, again and again, until His presence becomes our first instinct in every moment of fear.

Curl Up Close and Pray

Lord Jesus, thank You for being my Shepherd, the One I can run to whenever fear rises in my heart. Teach me to come to You quickly, honestly, and without shame. When life shakes me, when unexpected storms break across my world, when my heart trembles and I feel overwhelmed, help me remember that Your presence is my refuge. Let Your nearness calm my thoughts, steady my emotions, and quiet the fears that speak too loudly. Hold me close when I feel weak. Whisper peace into the places that panic tries to fill. And remind me again and again that I am never safer than when I am in Your arms. Thank You for loving me with a gentleness stronger than any storm. Amen.

- 13 -
The Dog Who Forgot Yesterday

Paws and Open Your Heart

There is something almost miraculous about the way a dog wakes up every morning as if the whole world has been reset. A dog doesn't carry yesterday into today. They don't wake up replaying mistakes, brooding over disappointments, or nursing grudges. They don't walk into the kitchen with guilt written across their face because they chewed something last night. They don't slink around feeling embarrassed because they barked too much, tracked in mud, or refused to come inside when you called. As far as they are concerned, the moment the sun rises, everything starts fresh.

You see it in the way they greet you first thing in the morning. Their tail begins wagging before their eyes are even fully open. They stretch, shake their fur, and then bounce toward you with the same excitement they had when they first met you. They're not remembering that you scolded them for getting into the trash yesterday. They're not rehearsing the fact that you were busy and didn't play as long as usual. They're not keeping score of how many times you asked them to stop barking at the mailman. Dogs live with a memory for love, but not for offense.

And oh, the freedom they walk in because of it.

If you've ever watched a dog who had a rough day, maybe they were anxious, or sick, or disobedient, or unusually restless, you'll notice that by the next morning, they're simply themselves again. They don't bring shame into the new day. They don't dwell on how they "should have behaved." They don't wonder whether you're still upset. They live as if the slate has been wiped clean overnight. They begin again without hesitation.

There is something holy in that instinct. Something deeply instructive. Something we humans, who often drag yesterday's failures into today's sunrise, desperately need to learn.

Dogs don't remember in the way we do. They don't catalog hurt. They don't store regret. They don't relive moments again and again, giving the past power over the present. If yesterday held trouble, they let it go. If yesterday held discipline, they accept it but don't internalize it. If yesterday held disappointment, they don't carry it into today's joy. Their hearts open wide again with every new morning.

And because of that, dogs remain some of the most joyful creatures God ever made. Their joy is not fragile. It isn't tangled up in fear of what happened or anxiety about what might happen. Their joy springs fresh each day because their hearts are unburdened.

If you've ever had a dog come trotting toward you with

yesterday's worry completely washed from their eyes, you know how freeing and disarming that simple trust can be. They believe, fully and sincerely, that today is a new day and that your love for them hasn't changed. They believe they are welcome. They believe they belong. They believe nothing is hanging over their head. They believe that whatever happened yesterday has already been left behind.

And in their simplicity, they reveal a truth wrapped in fur and innocence: a heart that refuses to hold onto yesterday is a heart that can live fully today.

Scripture to Sink Your Teeth Into

2 Corinthians 5:17 (AMP)
"Therefore if anyone is in Christ, he is a new creation [reborn and renewed by the Holy Spirit]; the old things [the previous moral and spiritual condition] have passed away. Behold, new things have come…"

Lesson To Chew On

If there is one thing most believers struggle with, sometimes quietly, sometimes constantly, it is the weight of yesterday. We carry it like a backpack filled with stones: regrets that still ache, mistakes we replay in our minds, memories we can't seem to let go of, sins we're forgiven of but still ashamed of, seasons we've left behind but still feel connected to through guilt or loss. Our minds hold onto things our hearts were never meant to carry forever. And slowly, without realizing it, we begin to live today through the lens of yesterday.

But a dog does something very different. A dog accepts correction when needed, but never wears shame. They experience failure, but never let it define the next moment. They receive discipline, but never interpret it as rejection. They experience disappointment, but never lose faith in the relationship. They make mistakes, sometimes the same mistakes, but they don't allow those mistakes to become their identity. A dog simply allows yesterday to pass away.

And in that simple daily rhythm, they quietly echo the promise of Scripture: "The old things have passed away... new things have come."

This is the heart of the Gospel, and yet it is one of the hardest truths for us to live. We know intellectually that God forgives us, but emotionally we sometimes struggle to believe that the slate is truly clean. We think back to moments we wish we could erase. We replay words we wish we had never said. We carry scars from decisions that still sting. We wake up remembering the heaviness of yesterday as if God didn't declare His mercies new every morning.

But God does not ask us to drag yesterday into today. He asks us to let it go.

When God forgives, He doesn't hold the past over our heads. He doesn't keep a quiet record in His back pocket to bring up later. He doesn't say, "I forgive you, but I'll still treat you differently because of what you did." His forgiveness is not partial; it is complete. His mercy is not measured; it overflows. His renewal is not symbolic; it is transformative. He makes us new, truly new, not just in theory, but in reality.

A dog lives in that kind of freedom without needing a theology book. Their clean-slate instinct mirrors a spiritual truth we often forget. They aren't weighed down by yesterday's failures, and because of that, they enter today fully, with joy, with hope, with openness, with trust. How much more were we meant to walk in that kind of renewed living?

When a dog forgets yesterday, they aren't ignoring reality; they're embracing relationship. They know who they belong to. They know who loves them. They know they are welcome. They trust that nothing from the past has altered their standing with the one they adore. And that trust frees them to live wholeheartedly today.

Imagine waking up tomorrow with that kind of spiritual clarity, knowing that because of Christ, yesterday truly has passed away. Imagine beginning your morning without replaying last week's missteps or worrying about old regrets. Imagine breathing in the freedom of God's mercy and living like a new creation, not because you feel new, but because God said you are new.

Dogs don't cling to what God has already released. Maybe it's time we stop clinging too.

Curl Up Close and Pray

Lord Jesus, thank You for the mercy that renews me each morning. Help me let go of yesterday, the regrets, the mistakes, the memories that cling too tightly. Teach me to live in the freedom You purchased for me. Let my heart awaken each day with the same openness and trust I see in a faithful dog who believes they are loved, welcomed, and unburdened. Help me rest in the truth that I am truly a new creation, and that the old has passed away because You have made all things new. Amen.

- 14 -
Unleashed Grace

Paws and Open Your Heart

There is a moment every dog owner knows, a moment when the leash is finally unhooked, and something inside the dog changes instantly. You can feel the shift even before they move. Their body tenses, their tail lifts, their eyes brighten, and then, freedom. They launch forward with that unmistakable burst of energy, that joyous sprint that says, "I'm free! Nothing is holding me back!" Some run in wide circles as fast as their legs will carry them, ears flapping wildly. Some explode into the open space ahead, as if they've been waiting all day for this one perfect moment. Others leap, twist, roll, bounce, and wiggle like joy itself has taken over their entire body. And no matter how many times you've seen it, something about that moment always makes you smile.

A dog on a leash can be content. They can enjoy the walk, love your company, and feel safe in your presence. But a dog unleashed taps into something deeper, something wild, joyful, and fully alive. There is no tension holding them back. No resistance pulling at their neck. No constraint telling them how far they can go. They are free to run, to explore, to live with a fullness that only freedom can unlock. And the beautiful thing is this: even unleashed, they often stop and look back at you, making sure you're still near, still watching, still sharing in their joy. Freedom doesn't make them forget you. If anything, it draws them closer in heart.

But an unleashed dog also trusts the one who set them free. They don't question whether you'll call them back. They don't wonder whether they're allowed to enjoy this moment. They simply embrace the gift. They live fully inside the space you've given them. They run with confidence because they know the freedom came from your hand.

And oh, the contrast between the dog whose leash is taut, pulling, straining, resisting, and the dog who has been released! A leashed dog may walk obediently, but tension still tugs at them. Their movement is limited. Their exploration is restrained. Their excitement is subdued. Even their joy feels measured. But when the leash unclips and falls away, the dog doesn't just move differently, they become different. Their whole body expresses the relief of freedom. Their spirit rises. Their instincts awaken. Their joy overflows.

Yet as wild as their joy may look, it isn't rebellion. It isn't disobedience. It isn't running away. It's simply freedom responding to love.

Some dogs, especially those who were once abandoned, confined, or mistreated, respond even more dramatically when the leash comes off. They run not just with excitement, but with gratitude. You can almost feel the thankfulness in the way they look over their shoulder, in the way they circle back to you mid-run, in the way they collapse at your feet afterward, panting and smiling, as if saying, "Thank you for trusting me. Thank you for giving me space to live."

And if you've ever stood in an open field watching a dog run free, feeling the wind shift around them, seeing the sun catch their fur as they leap with unrestrained joy, you've witnessed a living portrait of what grace looks like, not grace that merely restrains the worst in us, but grace that unleashes the best in us. For when a dog is set free, they do not use that freedom to leave you; they use it to live fully because of you. And within that picture lies a truth as deep as mercy itself.

Scripture to Sink Your Teeth Into

Galatians 5:1 (NIV)

"It is for freedom that Christ has set us free. Stand firm, then, and do not let yourselves be burdened again by a yoke of slavery."

Lesson To Chew On

Grace is one of the most beautiful gifts God ever gave, yet one of the hardest for many believers to truly live in. We understand forgiveness in theory, but we often live with leashes still wrapped around our souls, leashes of guilt, fear, shame, regret, legalism, and old wounds that whisper, "You can go this far, but no farther." Many people walk through life forgiven, yet not free. Saved, yet still bound. Loved, yet holding back. But grace was never meant to be a leash that restricts; it was meant to be the freedom that unleashes.

Galatians tells us plainly: "It is for freedom that Christ has set us free." Grace is not merely pardon, it is release. Release from the burden of proving ourselves. Release from the weight of what we used to be. Release from the need to earn love that has already been freely given. Release from sins that no longer define us. Release from the chains of fear that once controlled our steps. Grace doesn't ask us to walk carefully so we don't mess up; grace invites us to run joyfully because we belong.

But many believers hesitate to live in that freedom. They fear grace will make them reckless. They fear freedom means losing structure or direction. They fear that without a spiritual leash, they'll wander too far. Yet think of the dog who has learned to love and trust their master, when the leash comes off, they do not run away. They run free, but not far. They run joyfully, but not alone. They run fully, but always in the direction of the one they love.

Grace works the same way. It doesn't produce rebellion; it produces relationship. It doesn't make us want to flee from God; it makes us want to stay close. True grace doesn't lower the standard, it lifts the heart. It unleashes joy instead of fear, affection instead of anxiety, obedience instead of obligation. When grace is understood, sin loses its appeal because love has won the heart.

God's grace is not fragile. It isn't threatened by your weakness. It isn't withdrawn when you stumble. It isn't reduced when you doubt. Grace releases you from living like a dog who expects to be yanked backward at any moment. It invites you to live like the dog running free across the open field, unburdened, unafraid, unashamed, fully alive.

The enemy wants to keep us leashed to our past. He wants us to believe that our mistakes still hold power, that our failures disqualify us, that our weaknesses make us unworthy. But the Shepherd knows better. He loosens the leash not because He expects us to run away, but because He knows freedom will draw us closer. He unhooks the restraints that fear built. He removes the knots we tied with our own guilt. He sets us free in the fullest sense of the word, free to run, free to breathe, free to live, free to grow, free to love Him not out of fear, but out of delight.

Grace does not unleash chaos; it unleashes joy. It unleashes identity. It unleashes purpose. It unleashes the deep, God-given desire to walk in the light with the One who set us free. When you finally begin to live in that kind of grace, when you let go of the leash of yesterday, you discover what freedom was meant to feel like. You discover you were not set free to run away from God, but to run differently with God. Unleashed. Unburdened. Unafraid.

And just like the dog who sprints with every ounce of strength they have, occasionally circling back to you with laughter in their eyes, your soul begins to experience what it means to run in grace, free from the past, free from fear, and free to love the One who set you loose from everything that once held you back.

Curl Up Close and Pray

Lord Jesus, thank You for the grace that sets me free, not partially, not conditionally, but completely. Help me stop living as if I am still tethered to the things You have already released me from. Teach my heart to trust Your love enough to live without fear. Unhook the leashes of shame, guilt, regret, and striving, and let me run in the freedom You died to give me. Let Your grace makes me confident, not cautious; joyful, not anxious; close to You, not bound by fear of failing You. Thank You that true freedom doesn't push me away from You, it draws me closer to Your heart. Amen.

- 15 -
When the Bark Is Worse
Than the Bite

Paws and Open Your Heart

Every dog has a voice. Some bark with deep, booming confidence, the kind that shakes the windows and makes strangers wonder if a small bear lives inside your house. Others bark with high-pitched enthusiasm, sounding more like a squeaky toy than a guard dog. Some bark only when necessary, their warnings sharp but rare. Others bark at everything, the mailman, the wind, a leaf brushing across the porch, or the suspicious shadow of a trash can that has been sitting in the same place for five years. But all dogs, at one time or another, bark louder than their courage truly runs.

You can often see it in their posture. A dog might fling themselves forward, chest out and voice booming, only to jump backward the moment whatever they were barking at moves even an inch. They bark to sound brave, to feel brave, or sometimes simply because they are trying to convince themselves they are brave. Their bark becomes a protective instinct, a warning, a way of expressing uncertainty in a world that sometimes feels too big.

But here's the thing dog owners know well: a bark doesn't always match the heart behind it. Some of the loudest barkers are the gentlest souls. They bark not to threaten, but to cope. Not because they want to attack, but because they want to understand. Not because they're dangerous, but because they're anxious. Their bark is their armor, their shield, their attempt to make sense of what frightens or confuses them. And sometimes, when you step close and speak softly, the bark fades instantly, replaced by the trembling body of a dog who simply needed reassurance.

There is something deeply human in that. We, too, have moments when our "bark" grows louder than our true courage. We raise our voice when we feel threatened. We overreact when we feel insecure. We lash out when we feel vulnerable. We speak more sharply than we intended when our heart feels frightened or overwhelmed. And like a dog whose bark hides more fear than fury, our loudest reactions often come from our deepest uncertainties.

If you've ever approached a barking dog with patience, kneeling down, speaking gently, offering your hand, you've seen how quickly the storm inside them calms. They lean forward, sniff the air, tilt their head, and then soften, realizing the threat they feared was never real. It wasn't danger they were reacting to; it was emotion. And what they needed more than correction was comfort.

And isn't it beautiful how quickly a dog forgives you after barking at something that wasn't dangerous? They don't stew in embarrassment. They don't punish themselves for overreacting. They don't carry shame for misreading a situation. They simply move on, tail wagging, heart open, ready to be loved and to love again. Their ability to let go of fear, frustration, or confusion is one of the quiet miracles that dog owners witness daily.

A dog's bark might be worse than their bite, but their heart is almost always better than either. Their reactions might be loud, but their devotion runs deep. Their fears might show up dramatically, but their love remains steady. And in their tender, imperfect, honest way, they remind us of something true about ourselves: our loudest moments don't define us. Our hearts do.

Dogs don't stay stuck in the moment of barking. They don't replay it in their mind. They don't worry about what you think of them afterward. They simply come close again, trusting that you love them more than their reaction. And in that trust, they show us how to move forward from our own messy moments, not with shame, but with humility, grace, and the willingness to stay close to the One who loves us.

Scripture to Sink Your Teeth Into

Proverbs 15:1 (AMP)
"A soft and gentle and thoughtful answer turns away wrath, but harsh and painful words stir up anger."

Lesson To Chew On

We all have moments when our "bark" gets the best of us. Moments when we speak too quickly, react too strongly, or allow fear, stress, or insecurity to shape our tone more than wisdom or love. A sharp word slips out when we feel cornered. A defensive comment rises when we feel misunderstood. A harsh response tumbles out before we've had time to breathe, think, or pray. And afterward, we feel the sting of regret. We replay the conversation. We imagine the other person's hurt. We wish we could rewind time and choose gentleness instead.

But in those moments, we are not alone. Scripture acknowledges that human anger, fear, and impulsive reactions exist, and it offers a better way. "A gentle answer turns away wrath," Proverbs tells us, "but harsh words stir up anger." The verse is simple, but its wisdom is profound: gentleness disarms what harshness inflames. Softness calms what sharpness provokes. Patience heals what impatience harms.

A barking dog doesn't need someone to bark back; it needs someone who understands what's underneath the noise. Often, the bark hides insecurity. Sometimes it hides confusion. Other times it hides fear or overstimulation. Addressing the bark without addressing the heart leaves the struggle untouched. Only compassion brings change.

Humans operate similarly. Our loudest reactions rarely come from strength; they come from vulnerability. The person who speaks harshly is often overwhelmed. The person who interrupts is often anxious. The person who lashes out is often hurting. The person who raises their voice is often fighting fears they haven't learned to name. And just like a dog who barks louder when they don't know what else to do, we bark when our hearts feel unsteady.

But here is the hope: God sees the heart behind every bark. He sees the fear behind the anger, the exhaustion behind the frustration, the wounds behind the defensiveness. And instead of meeting our bark with punishment, He meets it with gentleness. He does not shame us for reacting; He heals what caused the reaction. His answer to our harshness is His kindness. His answer to our fear is His peace. His answer to our overreaction is His steadiness. His answer to our trembling soul is His unfailing love.

Grace is God kneeling down beside us while we're barking at shadows we barely understand. Grace is God saying softly, "I'm here. It's alright. Come close." Grace is God knowing our weaknesses and not withdrawing His affection. Grace is God calming the storm inside us, not condemning us for the noise we made along the way.

When we let that truth settle into our bones, something changes. We no longer run from God after our loud moments, we run to Him. We don't hide in shame; we seek healing. We don't define ourselves by our reactions; we let God define us by His love. And slowly, the more we experience His gentleness, the more our own hearts learn to respond gently, to others, and even to ourselves.

A dog who barked yesterday can still be calm today because their heart resets easily. We, too, can walk in the freedom of reset, not by ignoring our reactions, but by bringing them to the One who can make our hearts whole. God is not intimidated by our bark; He is committed to transforming our heart.

So when you find yourself reacting loudly, snapping, defending, barking at life, pause. Breathe. Let God kneel beside you. Let Him soften your spirit. Let His gentleness teach you how to answer gently. And remember that your bark does not define you. Your heart does. And your heart is being shaped by a Shepherd whose love is greater than your loudest moment.

Curl Up Close and Pray

Lord Jesus, thank You for understanding my heart even when my reactions are louder than my intentions. Help me grow in gentleness. Teach me to pause before I speak, to breathe before I react, and to choose compassion when my emotions feel overwhelming. Calm my fears, quiet my anxieties, and steady my spirit so that my words reflect Your love. Thank You for meeting my bark with grace instead of judgment. Help me show that same gentleness to the people around me, and to myself. Amen.

- 16 -
Guard Dog Strength

Paws and Open Your Heart

Every dog has a protective side, even the small ones who look more like walking teddy bears than fierce defenders. Some dogs stand tall at the first sign of trouble, their chest lifting, their body stiffening, and their eyes narrowing with that unmistakable "I'm on duty" intensity. Others react less dramatically but no less loyally, stepping in front of you, leaning against your leg, or giving a low warning rumble from deep inside their chest. And then there are the dogs who surprise you entirely: the quiet ones who rarely bark, but the moment a stranger approaches your home, their entire demeanor changes. They plant their paws, raise their head, and let loose a sound you didn't know their little body could make.

Guard dog behavior isn't always about size or breed; it's about devotion. Even a small dog with tiny legs and a squeaky bark will fling themselves into danger if they believe you need protecting. Their courage is not calculated. It isn't based on their odds of winning. They don't measure the threat or consider whether they're strong enough to handle it. They simply react out of loyalty. Their instinct says, "If you threaten my person, you go through me first."

And there is something remarkably moving about that, a love so fierce it forgets itself. A dog doesn't think, "This might hurt," or, "I'm too little for this." They simply stand their ground because protecting you isn't a duty, it's a devotion. It's built into their heart. Even the gentlest dog, the one who rolls over for belly rubs and sleeps with their paws twitching in dreams, can become a pillar of strength when they feel their family is in danger.

Sometimes the protection is loud and dramatic, a booming bark echoing through the hallway, a dance of paws and growls, a stance that says, "Stay back." Other times, it's quieter: the dog who follows you into every dark room, the one who sleeps with one ear open at night, or the one who sits beside you when you're sad as though guarding your heart instead of your home. Dogs don't just protect our bodies; they sense when our emotions need guarding too. They press close when they feel our sorrow. They lay their head on our lap when our spirit feels fragile. They stand between us and loneliness, between us and fear, between us and the heaviness the world can place on our shoulders.

Guard dog strength isn't always loud. Sometimes it's the quiet faithfulness of staying near. Sometimes it's the courage of stepping forward. Sometimes it's the calm presence that tells your heart, "You're safe." And if you've ever felt that moment, when your dog stands watch, not because they have to, but because they love you, you know what a profound comfort it is.

Because in their protective instincts, something holy is reflected. Something about the way they place themselves between you and danger whispers a truth we often forget: you were meant to be protected. You were meant to feel safe. You were meant to live under the covering of a love stronger than whatever stands against you. A dog guarding its owner is a small but powerful echo of the strength of a God who watches over His children with a devotion that never sleeps.

Scripture to Sink Your Teeth Into

Psalm 121:3–5, 7–8 (AMP)

3 He will not allow your foot to slip; He who keeps you will not slumber.

4 Behold, He who keeps Israel will neither slumber nor sleep.

5 The Lord is your keeper; the Lord is your shade on your right hand.

7 The Lord will protect you from all evil; He will keep your life.

8 The Lord will guard your going out and your coming in [everything that you do] from this time forth and forever.

Lesson To Chew On

There is a comfort we feel when a dog stands guard beside us, not because we believe they are invincible, but because we know their loyalty is absolute. They cannot control every danger, but they refuse to abandon their post. Their protective presence reminds us that we're not alone. That someone is watching. That someone cares deeply about our well-being. And what a beautiful reminder that is of the heart of God toward His people.

Psalm 121 paints a picture of divine protection that is steady, constant, and unwavering. "He who keeps you will not slumber… The Lord will guard your going out and your coming in… He will keep your life." That's not passive love, that's active, attentive, ever-present care. It is the picture of a God who stands watch over His children with a strength far beyond anything we could muster on our own. Not for a moment is He off-duty. Not for a moment does He look away. Not for a moment does He lose track of you.

We often forget that. Life gets loud. Danger feels close. Stress knots our shoulders. Worry curls around our thoughts like a fog. And before we realize it, we begin living as if protection is something we must create, something we must maintain, something we must guard with our own strength. But the truth is simpler, and far gentler: God is your Keeper. God is your Protector. God stands watch even when you sleep, even when you worry, even when you feel unsteady or small.

A dog guards with limited strength, but unlimited love. God guards with unlimited strength and perfect love.

Sometimes God's protection looks like shielding us from dangers we never even knew were near. Sometimes it looks like giving us wisdom to avoid trouble. Sometimes it looks like peace in the middle of chaos, the kind of peace that wraps around our heart like the steady presence of a dog sitting close on a stormy night. Sometimes His protection means stepping into battles we could not win on our own. And sometimes it means guarding our hearts from things that would have crushed us, had He not gently intervened.

But His protection is never passive. Never absent. Never uncertain. Just as a dog instinctively places itself between you and harm, God stands between you and every force that seeks to destroy your peace, your purpose, your hope, or your identity. When fear growls at your mind, God stands guard. When shame whispers its accusations, God shields you with truth. When sorrow presses in, God becomes your refuge. When spiritual attacks rise, God becomes your fortress. You are not watching the world alone, your Shepherd is watching over you.

And the more we learn to trust His guarding presence, the less fear dominates our hearts. We begin to walk with greater confidence. We breathe deeper. We rest more fully. We stop living like threatened creatures and begin living like beloved children, secure, held, and protected.

A dog's protective instinct is just a shadow. God's protective love is the true substance. His strength is perfect. His watchfulness is constant. His devotion is eternal. And just as your dog guards you out of love, God guards you out of a love infinitely deeper, a love that will never leave its post, never lower its shield, and never stop keeping your life.

Curl Up Close and Pray

Lord Jesus, thank You for being my Protector, my Keeper, and my constant Guardian. Thank You for watching over me when I am awake and when I sleep, when I am confident and when I am afraid, when I feel strong and when I feel fragile. Help me trust Your protection more deeply. Quiet the fears that whisper lies to my heart. Remind me that You stand between me and every danger, every threat, every dark thing that seeks to steal my peace. Let Your presence be my calm, Your strength be my safety, and Your love be the fortress around my life. Help me rest beneath Your watchful care, knowing that I am never unguarded and never alone. Amen.

- 17 -
When a Dog Brings You a Gift

Paws and Open Your Heart

Every dog owner has experienced it at least once, that unexpected moment when your dog trots toward you proudly carrying some kind of "treasure" in their mouth. It might be a stick, a shoe, a leaf, a sock, a favorite toy, or something baffling they dug up in the yard three years after you forgot it existed. Their tail is high, their eyes bright, their steps purposeful. They come to you not by accident, but with intention, holding their "gift" carefully and presenting it as if they've just returned from a grand adventure.

It doesn't matter whether the object has value to you. To them, it matters because they chose it for you. Sometimes the gift makes you laugh, like the time they dropped a slobbery tennis ball on your pillow at 6 a.m. Or the time they proudly brought in a stick so enormous it barely fit through the door and nearly took out a lamp on the way. Other times, the gift surprises you with its sweetness, when they pick up their favorite stuffed toy and drop it gently at your feet, as if saying, "This brings me joy... and I want to share it with you." And occasionally, the gift is more "nature-based" than you wished, a rock, a wad of grass, or the dreaded mystery item they found behind the shed. But regardless of what it is, the intention remains the same: they want to give you something because they love you.

A dog doesn't bring a gift because they think you need it. They bring a gift because their heart overflows. Their offering is not about usefulness; it is about affection. They are sharing the world as they understand it, the things they find interesting, comforting, or valuable. And that sharing is their way of saying, "I choose you. I belong to you. I delight in giving something to you."

Even more touching is the look they give afterward, that hopeful, tail-wagging glance that waits for your approval. Not approval of the item, but of them. They want to know that you receive their gift, that you see their heart behind it, that you appreciate the love they wrapped inside that slobbery stick or crumpled leaf. They want connection. They want closeness. They want to participate in your joy because you participate in theirs.

This instinct shows up in tender ways too. When you're sad and lying on the couch, they might bring their toy and place it near your hand, almost as if offering comfort. When you're busy or distracted, they might bring something just to remind you that they're there. When you've been gone longer than they hoped, they might greet you with a toy, circling you with excitement, eager to share their happiness with you. Dogs share what they love with the ones they love, and that simple act carries a depth of meaning we often overlook.

Because there's something beautiful in a creature who offers without agenda. Something pure in giving what little they have with wholehearted devotion. Something holy in the way they trust you to receive their offering even if it's imperfect. Their gift may be small, but their heart is large. And in their simple, cheerful generosity, their desire to offer you something that delighted them, we glimpse a living parable of love in its purest form: not polished, not impressive, but sincere, humble, and eager to give.

Scripture to Sink Your Teeth Into

1 Chronicles 29:14 (AMP)

"But who am I, and who are my people, that we should be able to offer as generously as this? For all things come from You, and from Your own hand we have given to You."

Lesson To Chew On

When a dog brings you a small "gift," it is easy to smile because the offering is so honest. It may be messy, imperfect, or puzzling, but it's given with sincerity, and you receive it because you love the giver. In that simple exchange lies a truth that cuts to the core of the Christian life: everything we offer God rests on that exact same dynamic. We give not because God needs anything, but because our hearts need to give.

We often complicate this idea. We worry about whether our offering is good enough, pure enough, big enough, polished enough. We think God is measuring the quality of our "gift" instead of the sincerity of our heart. We compare what we have to others, believing our contribution is too small, too simple, too ordinary. But Scripture reminds us that everything we give God, our time, our service, our worship, our finances, our obedience, our prayers, our attention, was first given to us by Him. We are not giving Him something He lacks; we are offering Him something He loves: a willing heart.

A dog bringing you a gift models something deeply spiritual. They bring what they have, not what they don't. They give cheerfully, not reluctantly. They offer joyfully, not fearfully. They give without shame, without comparison, without hesitation. Their offering may not be perfect, but their love is, and you receive it with affection because the value is in the giver, not the gift.

God relates to us the same way. He does not evaluate your offering based on worldly measurements. He does not compare your gift to another's. He does not criticize the size, polish, or perfection of what you bring. He delights in authenticity. He values sincerity. He cherishes willingness. He loves the relationship behind the offering more than the offering itself.

What if we learned to give like that? What if we offered God our time with the same excited wag that a dog has when offering a toy? What if we stopped overthinking whether our worship sounds good and simply offered it because we love Him? What if we stopped feeling embarrassed about small acts of obedience and began seeing them as beautiful? What if we stopped comparing our gifts to others and remembered that God smiles at our offering not because it is impressive, but because it is ours?

A dog does not bring you a gift to earn love; they bring it because they already have love. The same is true of us. We give not to earn God's approval, but because we already have it. We serve not to gain His affection, but because His affection has already been poured out. We offer what we have because He has offered us His heart.

A dog teaches us that giving is about joy, not pressure, about connection, not performance. Their gift is a bridge between hearts, an expression of affection, a simple declaration: "I love you, and I want to share something with you." And when we give to God with that same posture, humble, joyful, unselfconscious, we enter into the kind of offering He has always desired: one rooted in relationship rather than obligation.

Your gift, however small it may seem, delights Him. Your offering matters not because of what it is, but because of who gives it, His beloved child. And when you learn to give like a dog bringing its treasure, freely and gladly, you step into the divine joy of generosity, the joy of giving back from what God first placed in your hands.

Curl Up Close and Pray

Lord Jesus, thank You for receiving the simple offerings of my heart with love and joy. Help me give to You freely, not out of duty, but out of delight. Teach me to offer what I have without fear, without comparison, without trying to make it perfect. Let my giving flow from gratitude. Let my service flow from love. Let my acts of kindness, worship, and obedience be gifts laid at Your feet with sincerity. Thank You that what matters most to You is not the size of the offering, but the heart of the one who brings it. Make me generous, joyful, humble, and willing. Amen.

- 18 -
Where the Master Leads

Paws and Open Your Heart

Every dog knows the feeling of walking beside the one they love, that steady rhythm of footsteps, the gentle tug of the leash, the familiar sound of the voice they trust most. Walks aren't just exercise to a dog; they're communion. They're partnership. They're a moment shared between two lives traveling in the same direction. And it doesn't take long for a dog to learn the subtle language of the walk: the way your pace communicates something, the way your steps guide them, the way your voice anchors them, the way your presence defines their path.

Some dogs are natural followers, content to match your stride and stay close to your side. They don't need to know where they're going; they only need to know who they're going with. Others are enthusiastic explorers, always pulling ahead, always eager to discover something new, always tempted to run toward the next smell, the next sound, the next adventure. They check the length of the leash constantly, not out of rebellion, but out of excitement. And then there are the dogs who walk hesitantly, taking careful steps, glancing up at you often for reassurance, waiting for the signal that everything is safe.

But regardless of their personality, every dog walks better when they trust the one holding the leash. Trust changes everything. A dog who trusts their master will follow even when the path turns unexpectedly. They don't need explanations; they simply adjust. If you stop, they stop. If you turn, they turn. If you pause to look at something, they pause too, watching your face as if reading a silent message. They walk with confidence not because they know the way, but because they know the one who does.

And every dog owner knows the moment the leash slackens, that moment when the dog is no longer pulling, no longer resisting, no longer distracted by everything that tugs at their senses. The leash hangs loose, not because the walk has become dull, but because the dog has found the right rhythm, the rhythm of trust, alignment, and companionship. When a dog reaches that place, the walk becomes peaceful. The world around them may be full of distractions, but their focus narrows to the presence of the one leading them. It is a beautiful image of loyalty, and an even more powerful image of surrender.

Sometimes the most touching moments happen when the dog willingly slows down, matching your pace even when they could run ahead. They choose closeness over independence, presence over adventure. They walk not because the path is interesting, but because you are there. For them, the destination matters far less than the company. And if you've ever looked down to see your dog glancing up at you while walking, eyes soft, ears relaxed, steps steady, you know that what they want most is simply to stay near the one they love.

In their gentle devotion lies a truth we often overlook: following someone you trust isn't restrictive, it's freeing. It allows you to move through the world without fear, without pressure, without the constant burden of figuring out every turn. A dog walking beside their master is not confined; they are comforted. They are guided. They are anchored. And in their steady steps, we can see a reflection of the kind of walk the heart longs for, a walk where we don't have to lead, because we trust the One who does.

Scripture to Sink Your Teeth Into

Psalm 23:3 (AMP)
"He refreshes and restores my soul; He leads me in the paths of righteousness for His name's sake."

Lesson To Chew On

The Christian life is often described as a walk, a daily journey of following God step by step, pace by pace, moment by moment. But if we're honest, many believers spend their lives tugging at the leash. We pull ahead in impatience, wanting God to hurry up. We drift to the side in distraction, drawn by things that sparkle for a moment but lead nowhere meaningful. Or we drag behind in fear, hesitant to move forward into places God is calling us. And in all of it, God continues guiding with a gentle hand and a loving voice, inviting us to walk beside Him.

Psalm 23 reminds us that God doesn't drive us, He leads us. He doesn't push us from behind; He walks ahead of us, inviting us to follow. He doesn't shout orders from a distance; He stays close enough for us to sense His presence. And He doesn't lead us into places meant to harm us; He leads us into "paths of righteousness," paths that restore, strengthen, heal, and bring us into alignment with His heart.

But following God requires the same thing a dog demonstrates on a peaceful walk: trust. Trust that He knows where He's going. Trust that He won't abandon you midway. Trust that the path you're on is not an accident. Trust that even when the scenery changes suddenly, His hand has not let go. Trust that His pace, even when it feels slow, is intentional. Trust that every turn has purpose. Trust that His voice will be enough to steer your steps.

A dog doesn't always understand where you're going or why you stopped or why you turned left instead of right. But they understand you. And that's enough. What if we lived our walk with God the same way? What if we made peace with not always knowing the details? What if we trusted the Guide more than the map? What if we found rest in following instead of striving?

There is freedom in surrendering the need to lead. There is peace in letting God set the pace. Some seasons He walks slowly, giving your soul time to breathe. Other seasons He leads quickly, pushing you forward into growth you didn't know you were ready for. And sometimes, He pauses, not because He's uncertain, but because you need rest. If we learn to stay close, we will discover that His timing is not just right, it is perfect.

And here is something beautiful: God doesn't require perfect obedience to keep walking with us. He doesn't yank harshly when we stray, nor does He abandon us when we pull too hard. He gently guides us back, patiently teaching us His rhythm until our steps begin to match His. Over time, the leash slackens, not because God's expectations lessen, but because our trust increases. We learn to walk in harmony with Him.

A dog who walks beside their master is not driven by fear; they are shaped by relationship. And the same is meant to be true for us. The Christian walk isn't meant to be a series of forced steps, it is meant to be a journey of companionship with the Shepherd who loves us. He invites us, leads us, protects us, and stays beside us in every season.

When we learn to walk where the Master leads, life becomes less about striving and more about abiding. Less about anxiety and more about trust. Less about control and more about closeness. And in that closeness, we find the joy of knowing that wherever He leads, even through valleys, even through uncertainties, His presence makes every step safe.

Curl Up Close and Pray

Lord Jesus, teach me to walk with You in trust and peace. Help me stop tugging at the leash, stop rushing ahead, and stop falling behind. Align my steps with Yours. Let me feel Your presence guiding me, comforting me, and leading me into paths that restore my soul. Make me sensitive to Your voice and steady in Your direction. Help me trust Your pace, Your timing, and Your wisdom. And above all, keep me close, walking beside You, following where You lead, and resting in the assurance that I am safe in Your hands. Amen.

- 19 -
The Dog Who Waits by the Door

Paws and Open Your Heart

There is a moment, familiar to nearly every dog owner, when you stand on the other side of the door, whether coming home from a long day, a short errand, or even just a trip to the mailbox, and there your dog is, waiting as if the universe has been holding its breath until the very moment you walk back into view. The waiting varies from dog to dog, but the heart behind it is the same. Some sit upright, ears perked, watching the door with quiet expectation. Others lie down with their head on their paws, rising the second they hear the faintest sound of your return. And then there are the excitable ones, the tail thumpers, the window watchers, the ones who pace with anticipation, convinced that every car is yours, every sound belongs to you, every moment is the moment you'll come back.

What touches the heart most deeply is the unwavering certainty they have that you will come back. Their waiting is not anxious or doubtful. They do not sit at the door chewing their nails, worrying you have forgotten them. They wait with a peaceful kind of hope, the kind that believes wholeheartedly that love always returns. No matter how long you've been gone, whether minutes or hours, your dog's confidence never changes. They are sure of your love. They are sure of your presence. They are sure of your return. And that certainty shapes their entire demeanor.

Sometimes their waiting is patient. Other times it's restless, especially when your absence feels longer than usual. Some dogs whine softly. Some pace. Some leave the door for a moment, only to come right back again. But they always return to wait because their hearts anchor themselves to the one they love. You are their home, and if home is not in sight, they wait at the door where it will soon appear.

Their waiting is filled with devotion. They don't pass the time planning how upset they'll be with you for leaving. They're not preparing a cold shoulder or a guilt trip. They're preparing joy. The moment the doorknob turns, their entire body reacts, tails wag furiously, paws dance, eyes brighten, and sometimes they greet you with a toy, a bark, or a full-body wiggle that communicates excitement in a language beyond words. Their waiting gets rewarded with reunion, and their reunion is always marked by love.

Dogs do not grow bitter when you are gone. They do not resent the time or distance. They simply long for connection, and their longing is pure. They wait because you matter to them more than anything else in the moment. And their waiting reveals a depth of loyalty few creatures on earth express so consistently, so faithfully, so joyfully.

If you've ever paused a moment before entering, just to watch your dog's ears perk up, or to see the shadow of their tail swishing under the doorframe, you know how powerful this little picture is. It's not about routine. It's about relationship. That waiting dog, full of hope, full of love, full of expectation, is a living reminder of a truth we sometimes forget in our busy, burdened lives: love inspires hope, and hope inspires waiting.

A dog's waiting is not passive or empty. It is an act of love. It is a gift of loyalty. It is their way of saying, "You matter to me. I expect you. I want you. I will be here when you come." And in that simple, faithful posture, they show us something profoundly spiritual, something about hope, perseverance, longing, and the expectation of reunion.

They wait because their heart is tied to yours. And when love ties itself to someone, waiting becomes natural.

Scripture to Sink Your Teeth Into

Psalm 130:5–6 (AMP)
"I wait [patiently] for the Lord, my soul [expectantly] waits, and in His word do I hope. My soul waits for the Lord more than the watchmen for the morning..."

Lesson To Chew On

Waiting is one of the hardest things God ever asks us to do. We wait for answers, for healing, for direction, for breakthrough, for clarity, for peace, for open doors, for closed wounds, for restored relationships, for new opportunities, for old fears to fade, for prayers to be fulfilled. And if we are honest, human waiting often feels heavy. It is full of questions, doubts, fears, and impatience. We wonder how long it will take. We wonder why it hasn't happened yet. We wonder if God heard us. We wonder if we misunderstood His promise. We wonder if we are doing something wrong or missing something important. We wait, but we do not always wait well.

And yet Scripture calls us to a different kind of waiting, the kind that looks more like a dog waiting at the door than a person pacing the floor. It calls us to wait with expectation rather than anxiety. With hope rather than dread. With trust rather than fear. With confidence rather than despair. "My soul waits for the Lord," the psalmist writes, "more than watchmen wait for the morning." And that kind of waiting is not worried about whether the sun will rise, it is only watching for when it will rise.

A dog waiting at the door teaches us that waiting is easier when love is the foundation. They wait, not because they fear abandonment, but because they are assured of belonging. They wait with joy because they are confident in reunion. Their waiting is rooted in relationship, not insecurity. What if our waiting for God looked like that? What if we waited with the assurance that God always keeps His word, always returns, always fulfills His promises? What if we waited with the certainty that He has never once failed to show up?

Our frustration in waiting often comes from forgetting who we are waiting for. We focus on the problem instead of the Person. We fix our eyes on the delay instead of the Deliverer. We stare at the closed door instead of the One who will eventually open it. But waiting becomes a different experience when we remember that God is faithful, not occasionally, not sometimes, but always.

And perhaps the most beautiful part of waiting like a dog is this: their waiting is not bitter. They don't resent the delay. They don't punish you for returning later than expected. They don't sulk or withdraw in coldness. They explode with joy the instant you walk through the door, as if the waiting only intensified their love. That is how Scripture describes waiting on God: "Those who wait on the Lord shall renew their strength." Waiting with trust doesn't drain us; it restores us.

God never wastes waiting. Waiting seasons stretch our faith, sharpen our ears, strengthen our hearts, deepen our dependence, and prepare us for the blessing ahead. Sometimes the delay is not punishment, it is preparation. Sometimes it is protection. Sometimes it is positioning. Sometimes it is pruning. But it is never abandonment. God is not ignoring you. He is working in ways you cannot yet see, and when the moment is right, He will walk through the "door" of your situation with perfect timing.

A dog waits for its master because love assures them the master will return. We wait for God because His character assures us the same. He has never failed to come through. He has never broken a promise. He has never left a child waiting forever.

And when He comes, when the door finally opens, all the waiting will make sense, and joy will overflow.

Curl Up Close and Pray

Lord Jesus, teach me to wait with hope, not fear. Help me trust Your timing when mine fails. Remind me that waiting is not a sign of abandonment, but a sign that You are working behind the scenes. Give my heart the patience of a dog waiting at the door, confident, expectant, full of trust. Anchor my soul to Your faithfulness. Strengthen me when the waiting feels long. And help me greet Your answers with joy, knowing that You always return, always arrive, always come through. Amen.

- 20 -
A Dog's Kind Eyes

Paws and Open Your Heart

If you've ever paused long enough to truly look into a dog's eyes, really look, you know there is a quiet kindness there that words can hardly describe. A dog's eyes can soften even the hardest days. They have a way of looking straight through the noise, the stress, the busyness, and the mess of life, and seeing you, not your mistakes, not your mood, not your imperfections. Just you. Their eyes carry a gentleness that seems to whisper,

"You're safe with me. I'm glad you're here. I love you exactly as you are." In a world filled with judgment, pressure, comparison, and endless expectations, the simple kindness of a dog's gaze is a rare and healing gift.

A dog doesn't look at you differently when your hair is messy, when you're wearing old clothes, or when your day has worn you thin. They don't evaluate your expression before deciding whether to greet you. They don't check your mood first. They look at you the same, with affection, excitement, tenderness, and trust. Their eyes light up because you exist. That's enough for them. And somehow, standing in that gaze, you feel seen in a way that is pure and unfiltered, uncomplicated and unconditional.

There is honesty in a dog's eyes. They don't hide their emotions or disguise their devotion. Their eyes reveal delight when you walk through the door. They reveal concern when you're upset. They reveal compassion when you're hurting. They reveal loyalty when you're unsure. They reveal forgiveness even when you've been frustrated with them. Their eyes reflect their heart, and their heart is overwhelmingly kind.

Sometimes, on the hardest days, when the world feels sharp or cold, a dog's eyes can stop you in your tracks. You can be overwhelmed, exhausted, frustrated, or discouraged, and suddenly there they are, looking up at you with soft, steady affection as if saying, "It's okay. I'm here." You may not have said a word about your struggles, but they sense something. They lean in closer. Their gaze lingers. They communicate a comfort deeper than language. And in that moment, something in you exhales.

A dog's kind eyes don't fix life's problems, but they soften life's edges. They don't eliminate stress, but they make the moment feel lighter. They don't remove sorrow, but they bring a glimmer of companionship into the heaviness. They look at you with a love so uncomplicated that you find yourself wondering why humans struggle so much to love with such gentleness. A dog isn't keeping record of wrongs. A dog isn't deciding whether you deserve affection today. A dog isn't withholding kindness because of something that happened yesterday. Their eyes hold no grudge, no resentment, no distance. Their eyes say, "You are loved. Right now. As you are."

And maybe the most touching part is this: dogs don't reserve that kindness for your best days. They show it on all your days. Days you're happy. Days you're irritable. Days you're sad. Days you're busy. Days you're distracted. Days you fail. Days you struggle. Days you don't feel like yourself. Their eyes stay soft because their love stays steady.

If you've ever knelt down beside your dog, placed your hand gently on the side of their face, and looked into those warm eyes, you know the peace that flows from that moment. It's not dramatic. It's not loud. It's not complicated. It's simply connection, pure, honest, unconditional connection. And in that connection, you catch a glimpse of something divine.

Scripture to Sink Your Teeth Into

Psalm 33:18 (AMP)
"Behold, the eye of the Lord is upon those who fear Him [with awe-inspired reverence and obedience], those who hope confidently in His compassion."

Lesson To Chew On

There is something profoundly healing about the way a dog looks at you with kindness. Their eyes do not judge or accuse.

They do not reflect disappointment. They do not search for flaws. They hold only affection and loyalty. And while a dog's love is a beautiful gift, it is only a faint echo of a far greater truth, the kindness of the way God looks at you.

Many believers struggle with how they imagine God's gaze. We picture Him looking at us through the lens of our failures: stern, disappointed, weary of our mistakes. We imagine Him shaking His head at our inconsistency, frustrated by our weakness, distant because of our imperfections. But that is not the gaze Scripture describes. The Bible tells us, "The eye of the Lord is upon those who hope confidently in His compassion." God looks at His children through the lens of compassion, not condemnation. His gaze is not harsh; it is kind. Not cold; warm. Not critical; loving.

That truth, if truly understood, could transform a person's entire walk with God.

Imagine looking up and seeing God's eyes filled not with anger, but with affection. Imagine seeing His gaze steady and patient, not demanding that you be perfect, but inviting you to rest in His love. Imagine realizing that the One who knows everything about you, every flaw, every failure, every insecurity, looks at you with the same kind of tenderness that softens your heart when your dog gazes up at you. Only deeper. Only purer. Only perfect.

A dog's kind eyes remind us that love sees the heart, not the performance. God's gaze works the same way. He sees you, not who you pretend to be, not who you fear you are, but who He made you to be. And He looks at you with compassion every time. When you're tired, His gaze is gentle. When you're lost, His gaze is guiding. When you're ashamed, His gaze is forgiving. When you're broken, His gaze is compassionate. When you're lonely, His gaze is present. His eyes are on you not to scrutinize you, but to shepherd you.

We spend so much time fearing God's disappointment that we forget He delights in His children. We fixate on our weaknesses and forget His kindness. We brace ourselves for judgment and miss His mercy. But if a dog can look at us with consistent affection, how much more must the God who created love Himself look upon us with kindness far beyond what a creature could ever show?

When God looks at you, He sees someone worth loving. Worth saving. Worth redeeming. Worth shaping. Worth holding close. His gaze isn't searching for reasons to pull away; it's filled with reasons He draws near.

A dog's kind eyes can melt a stressed heart. God's loving gaze can heal a wounded soul.

Let this truth settle deeply: God does not see you with harshness. He sees you with compassion. And if we begin to trust His gaze, to really believe that He looks at us with love instead of condemnation, it changes everything. It changes how we pray. It changes how we confess. It changes how we worship. It changes how we view ourselves. It changes how we walk through life. For when you know you are seen with kindness, you walk with confidence instead of fear.

Dogs teach us many things, but perhaps this lesson is among the greatest: a gentle gaze has power. If a dog's kind eyes can bring comfort, imagine the healing hidden in God's.

Curl Up Close and Pray

Lord Jesus, thank You for looking at me with eyes full of compassion. Help me see myself the way You see me, loved, valued, forgiven, and held. Remove the fear that imagines Your gaze is harsh, and replace it with the truth of Your kindness. Let Your eyes be my comfort on the hard days and my hope on the lonely ones. Teach me to trust Your love more deeply than my failures. Help me walk in the confidence that I am always seen, always known, and always cherished by You. Amen.

- 21 -
Naps and Sabbath Rest

Paws and Open Your Heart

There is nothing quite like watching a dog sleep. It is one of the purest pictures of peace in all of creation. A dog does not worry about tomorrow or replay the mistakes of yesterday. They do not lie awake imagining worst-case scenarios or carrying the invisible weight that humans so often shoulder. When a dog sleeps, they surrender their entire body to rest, completely, unapologetically, wholeheartedly. Their breathing deepens, their muscles soften, their paws twitch in dreams, and their tail sometimes gives a faint, joyful wag as if even their subconscious knows what it means to rest without fear. They close their eyes with absolute confidence that the world will keep turning while they sleep. They trust the house around them, the people who love them, and the presence of their master nearby. They do not resist rest. They embrace it.

Sometimes a dog sleeps curled tightly in a ball, tucked into the corner of a couch cushion or nestled against your feet as if your nearness makes their rest sweeter. Other times they sleep sprawled across the floor with legs stretched out in all directions, belly exposed, a position of vulnerability that reveals how safe they feel in your presence. A dog does not hide when it is tired. It does not pretend it can keep going endlessly. It simply yields to exhaustion and lies down. It listens to the voice of its body without shame or guilt. And the moment sleep comes, their entire being seems to sigh.

What is remarkable is how often a dog will choose to rest not in a bed of its own, but beside the one it loves. They will curl up under your desk while you work, or beside you on the couch, or at the foot of the bed, or even in the doorway just to be near you. Rest is not merely a physical act for them; it is relational. They rest better when they are close to you. Your presence becomes their peace. The rhythm of your breathing becomes the rhythm of their calm. The steady sound of your steps or the gentle murmur of your voice assures them that all is well, even before sleep closes their eyes.

There is a lesson hidden in the way dogs nap throughout the day. They do not wait until they are completely depleted. They rest whenever their body needs rest. A beam of sunlight stretches across the floor, warm and inviting, and a dog will settle right into it without hesitation. A quiet afternoon comes, and while humans keep working, pushing, rushing, and filling their minds with constant activity, the dog simply stretches out and receives rest as a gift. They do not consider it wasted time. They do not view it as weakness. Rest is as natural to them as breathing.

And if you've ever had a dog fall asleep with its head resting against your leg, completely trusting you to watch over it, you know the sweetness of that moment. There is something almost holy about it, this simple creature, full of joy and loyalty, entrusting its entire rest into your care. It is a picture of peace, vulnerability, belonging, and security all wrapped into one.

A dog at rest reminds us of something we tend to forget: rest is not a luxury. It is not optional. It is not something we earn. It is something we need. It is something we were created for. And in a world that glorifies exhaustion and praises busyness, the peaceful surrender of a dog taking a nap becomes a gentle sermon in fur and paws, preaching a truth we desperately need to remember: rest is a sacred gift.

Scripture to Sink Your Teeth Into

Exodus 33:14 (AMP)
"And the Lord said, 'My presence shall go with you, and I will give you rest.'"

Lesson To Chew On

There is something deeply spiritual about learning to rest, because rest requires trust. It requires releasing control, letting go of striving, and believing that God is still in charge while you close your eyes. In many ways, the Sabbath is not about stopping work, it is about remembering who really holds the world. When we rest, we are declaring with our actions that God does not need our frantic effort to keep His universe functioning. He invites us to stop, breathe, pause, and remember Him.

Dogs teach this lesson beautifully because they do not carry the burdens we carry. They are not driven by the pressure to produce, achieve, or stay busy. They are not enslaved to the constant noise of the mind. They simply rest when they need rest, because they trust their environment, their provision, and their master. In a way, their naps are tiny declarations of faith. Rest means, "I am safe." Rest means, "I am provided for." Rest means, "Someone else is watching over me."

Humans, on the other hand, often struggle to surrender to stillness. We feel guilty for resting. We feel behind when we pause. We measure our worth by productivity, forgetting that God Himself rested on the seventh day, not because He was tired, but because rest is part of His design for creation. Sabbath was not made to restrict us. It was made to restore us.

In Exodus 33, God makes a profound promise: "My presence shall go with you, and I will give you rest." Rest is not found in the absence of responsibility, it is found in the presence of God. Just as a dog rests more peacefully when it is near the one it loves, our souls rest more deeply when we draw near to Jesus. His presence quiets the anxious mind. His nearness soothes the weary spirit. His voice calms the restless heart.

True rest is not simply physical sleep. It is spiritual peace, the kind that comes from knowing you are held, protected, loved, and provided for. You can lie down without fear because the Good Shepherd is watching over you. You can breathe deep because the One who never slumbers is guarding your life. You can stop striving because Jesus invites the weary: "Come to Me, and I will give you rest."

But many of us resist rest because we do not trust God fully. We think things will fall apart if we stop. We believe the world depends on our effort. We worry that if we slow down, everything will crumble. But resting is not irresponsibility, it is worship. It is obedience. It is a declaration of trust.

A dog lies down confidently because it knows it is safe. Shouldn't we, children of the Almighty, trust our Father even more?

When you allow yourself to rest, you are saying, "God, You are in control. My life is in Your hands. My future is secure in Your plan. My heart can lie down because You are awake. I can rest because You remain faithful."

Dogs teach us a sacred simplicity: rest is an act of trust in the love that surrounds you. When you learn to rest in God the way a dog rests beside its owner, your soul discovers the quiet, unshakable peace He has been offering you all along. Sabbath becomes more than a day, it becomes a posture of the heart, a way of living that trusts God enough to breathe deeply and rest freely in His presence.

Curl Up Close and Pray

Lord Jesus, teach my heart to rest. Help me lay down the burdens I was never meant to carry. Let Your presence calm my spirit the way my presence comforts the dog who loves me. Slow my mind, quiet my worries, and draw me near enough to hear You whisper peace into my soul. Thank You for being the One who watches over me so faithfully that I can rest without fear. Help me treat rest not as weakness but as worship, trusting that You hold my life securely in Your hands. Amen.

- 22 -
Learning New Tricks

Paws and Open Your Heart

There's an old saying people like to repeat: "You can't teach an old dog new tricks." Anyone who has ever loved a dog knows that isn't true. Dogs, whether young and curious or gray-muzzled and slow, remain surprisingly willing to learn, change, and grow if the one teaching them is someone they trust. There is something wonderfully hopeful about that. A dog, no matter its age, holds this quiet belief that life can still offer something new, that it is never too late to try, to grow, or to adapt. It shows in the way their ears perk up when you call their name with a new tone. It shows in the way they tilt their head when they hear a new command. It shows in the way they attempt something unfamiliar, often with clumsy enthusiasm, uncertain footing, and wagging courage.

Training a dog is not about perfection, it's about relationship. You see this every time they attempt a new trick. They may confuse "spin" with "sit" or "paw" with "down," but they are trying. Their tail wags as if to say, "I don't quite understand, but I'm doing my best because I want to please you." There is a humility and innocence in the way they learn. They listen, watch, attempt, fail, try again, and keep going because their desire to connect is stronger than their fear of getting it wrong.

You can almost feel their determination when they lock their eyes on you, waiting for some sign of approval, a smile, a gentle nod, a word of encouragement. They learn not because they fear punishment, but because they love the one who teaches them. And when they finally get it, when the trick clicks in their mind and they respond correctly, they light up with joy, almost as brightly as you do. Their excitement spills out of them, often in the form of jumps, wiggles, delighted barks, and a proud trot around the room. Success for them isn't about performing perfectly; it's about the joy of making you happy.

What is even more beautiful is how patient dogs are with themselves. They don't quit because they stumble. They don't call themselves failures because they misunderstood. They don't hide in shame because it took them a while to learn. They simply stay beside you, trusting that the process is good, that the teacher is kind, and that each new attempt moves them closer to understanding. There is something deeply inspiring in that kind of steady, hopeful effort.

And maybe that's why watching a dog learn something new stirs something inside us. It reminds us that growth is not about age or background or perfection. It reminds us that mistakes are not final. It reminds us that the process of learning, whether slow or fast, simple or difficult, is an expression of relationship, not pressure. A dog will try again simply because it loves you. And that love makes even the hardest lessons easier.

If you've ever bent down, looked into your dog's eyes, and said, "Let's try again," you know the sweetness of that moment. Their tail thumps the ground. Their body shifts forward with renewed hope. They are ready, even if they weren't a moment ago. Because your voice has a way of reviving their courage. Your encouragement has a way of stirring their confidence. Your presence makes the impossible feel possible.

Dogs are not afraid of learning new tricks. They are only afraid of being alone. As long as you are with them, they are willing. As long as you are encouraging them, they will try. As long as your love surrounds them, they believe that new things are still possible. And in their gentle, steady way, they teach us something beautiful about the courage it takes to learn, the humility it takes to grow, and the love that makes both worthwhile.

Scripture to Sink Your Teeth Into

Isaiah 43:18–19 (AMP)
"Do not remember the former things, nor ponder the things of the past. Listen carefully, I am about to do a new thing; now it will spring forth; will you not be aware of it?"

Lesson To Chew On

Dogs remind us that learning is not about perfection, it is about willingness. It is about staying close to the one who teaches, trusting the process, accepting our mistakes, and stepping into something new with courage. Spiritually, people often believe that change is impossible for them, especially if they've carried the same habits, wounds, patterns, or fears for years. They think, "I'll always be this way," or, "It's too late for me," or, "Maybe God can change others, but I'm stuck." But those lies crumble when held up to the light of Scripture, because God specializes in "new things." He does not simply improve the old. He transforms. He rebuilds. He renews. He resurrects. There is no age limit, no expiration date, and no disqualification for spiritual growth. If a dog can learn at twelve what it never learned at two, imagine what the Holy Spirit can do with a willing heart at any stage of life.

Isaiah 43 reveals God's heart: "Do not remember the former things... I am about to do a new thing." God is not interested in chaining you to your past. He is not limited by your old patterns. He is not discouraged by how long something has held onto you. He is the God who makes streams in the desert and pathways in the wilderness, which means He creates possibilities in places where none existed before. When you walk with Him, new things are not only possible, they are promised.

But learning something new spiritually requires the same posture we see in a dog learning a new trick. It requires humility, the willingness to say, "Lord, I don't have this figured out." It requires patience, accepting that growth may come slowly, unevenly, and sometimes with setbacks. It requires trust, believing that God is not frustrated with your progress, but delighted by your desire to grow. And it requires closeness, staying near to the One who teaches, because His presence is what empowers change.

Many believers quit too early because they imagine God as a harsh instructor, disappointed when they fail. But God is not like that. He is gentle. He is patient. He is encouraging. When you stumble, He doesn't scold you. He says, "Let's try again." When you misunderstand, He doesn't withdraw. He stays near and speaks clearer. When you feel too old, too broken, too flawed, or too far gone, He reminds you that His mercies are new every morning. New mercies for new growth. New grace for new beginnings. New strength for new steps.

A dog does not learn because it fears punishment, it learns because it trusts love. And when you learn to trust God's love in the same way, spiritual growth stops feeling like pressure and starts feeling like companionship. God walks with you. He teaches patiently. He celebrates progress. And He never gives up on you.

The truth is simple but profound: if you are still breathing, God is still teaching. If your heart is still beating, God is still shaping. If you are still alive, God is still ready to do a new thing in you. Whether it is healing an old wound, breaking a long-standing habit, strengthening a weak place, renewing your mind, reshaping your identity, or calling you into something you never believed you could do, God is not finished with you. Not by a long shot.

Dogs show us a beautiful picture of this truth. They do not know the full plan. They do not understand every command. But they trust the one who leads them. And because of that trust, they learn. They grow. They change. And if a creature of fur and paws can do that simply by trusting its master, how much more can a child of God learn, grow, change, and flourish by trusting the One who created them?

Curl Up Close and Pray

Lord Jesus, teach me to trust You in the process of growth. Help me believe that You truly can do new things in me, no matter my age, past, or struggles. Give me a humble heart that is willing to learn, a patient spirit that does not quit when I fall short, and a deep confidence in Your gentle, faithful love. Shape me, train me, and guide me step by step into the person You are calling me to be. Amen.

- 23 -
When You Wander Off

Paws and Open Your Heart

Every dog owner knows that sinking feeling that hits the moment you realize your dog has wandered away. One minute they are in the yard, sniffing happily, tail waving like a little flag in the sunlight. The next minute, the yard is too quiet. You call their name. You whistle. You listen for the jingle of their collar. Nothing. Just stillness. Your heart tightens. You step outside and scan the edges of the fence, the tree line, the driveway, hoping to catch a glimpse of movement, a flash of fur, anything at all. Dogs don't always wander off with rebellious intent. Sometimes a scent pulls them one step too far. Sometimes curiosity draws them beyond the familiar boundary. Sometimes a distraction lures them into forgetting where home is for just a moment. They don't mean to make you worry, they simply lose track of where they are.

When a dog wanders, you can almost picture the moment it realizes it has gone too far. There is a pause, a little uncertainty in their stance, their ears turning backward as if listening for a familiar voice. They look around, and suddenly everything feels strange. The world that seemed exciting a minute ago now feels bigger than they expected. The smell that led them here is gone. The yard looks distant. The house is out of sight. The thrill fades, and confusion settles in. It's in that moment, that moment of wrong turns and uncertain steps, that the longing for home is awakened.

A wandering dog doesn't usually run in a straight line once fear sets in. They pace. They turn in circles. They retrace their steps and then second-guess themselves. They perk up at every sound, hoping that the breeze might carry their owner's voice. They may even sit down for a moment, unsure of which way to go. And then something beautiful happens. They hear the voice they know best. Maybe it's faint at first, carried on the wind. Maybe it's strong and clear, echoing down the road. But the moment they hear it, their heart leaps. Their ears lift. Their body snaps to attention. That voice, the one that fed them, comforted them, protected them, loved them, cuts through every bit of confusion. And suddenly they remember who they belong to.

The run back home is rarely graceful. They stumble. They slip. They take awkward, hurried steps. Their body bounces with relief, tail spinning like a little propeller. They run not because they're afraid of punishment but because home is where their joy lives. They run because the voice that calls them is the voice of love. And when they finally reach you, panting, trembling, exhausted with both fear and relief, they press their head against your leg, lean their full weight into you, and breathe deeply as if to say, "I'm home. Thank you for calling me."

As a dog owner, the moment you see them again, something in your heart relaxes. The fear dissolves instantly into relief. You kneel down, wrap your arms around them, and feel their body soften against yours. You don't scold first. You hold first. The joy of reunion overwhelms the frustration of the wandering. The love outweighs the fear. The relief drowns out the worry. Because the return matters more than the wandering ever did.

The truth is simple: even when dogs wander, they never stop being yours. They may get confused. They may lose their way. They may chase the wrong thing. But the moment you call, everything in them turns homeward. And that moment, that beautiful turning, reveals a truth far deeper than the story of a wandering dog. It reveals the heart of longing, the pull of belonging, and the unshakeable bond between love and home.

Scripture to Sink Your Teeth Into

Luke 15:4–6 (AMP)

"What man among you, if he has a hundred sheep and loses one of them, does not leave the ninety-nine in the open pasture and go after the one that is lost until he finds it? And when he has found it, he lays it on his shoulders, rejoicing. And when he gets home, he calls together his friends and his neighbors, saying to them, 'Rejoice with me, because I have found my sheep which was lost!'"

Lesson To Chew On

Wandering is part of the human experience. We do not always stay near the Shepherd. Sometimes our hearts follow a distraction, something that looks harmless at first but slowly pulls us farther than we meant to go. Sometimes it is sin. Sometimes it is discouragement. Sometimes it is fear. Sometimes it is the slow drift of neglect, a quiet cooling of devotion, a hurried life that forgets the presence of God. And just like a dog caught up in curiosity, we often do not realize how far we've wandered until we suddenly feel lost, lonely, and unsure of how to find our way back.

The good news, the life-changing good news, is that Jesus is the kind of Shepherd who goes after the wandering ones. He does not wait for us to fix ourselves or find our own way home. He does not sit on the porch with crossed arms, tapping His foot, waiting to scold us. He comes looking. He calls our name. His voice echoes into the distant places we drifted into, speaking through Scripture, through sermons, through songs, through quiet whispers in our soul. He calls us not with anger but with love. Not with condemnation but with compassion. Not with impatience but with longing.

Jesus understands the heart that wanders. He understands how easily human beings get distracted by lesser things. He knows how loud the world can be and how quick we are to follow our own impulses. And yet, His love remains steady. The Shepherd's heart is not offended by our wandering, it is moved by it. He sees us vulnerable, confused, threatened by things we don't understand, and His compassion draws Him toward us, not away from us.

Wandering does not disqualify you from God's love; it awakens His pursuit.

When the lost sheep is found, Jesus says the Shepherd lifts it onto His shoulders and carries it home. That is not the image of a frustrated God. That is the image of overwhelming grace. The Shepherd does not walk behind the sheep, driving it with stern commands. He carries it, close to His heart, showing that restoration is not a punishment but a celebration. The return is what matters. The reunion is what brings joy. Heaven is not silent when a wanderer comes home; it rejoices.

The dog who wanders off and then runs back when it hears your voice is a small reflection of a greater truth: the human heart was created to come alive at the sound of God's call. When you feel lost, confused, tired, or guilty, listen for His voice. It is calling you back, not to shame you but to restore you. Not to expose you but to embrace you. Not to punish you but to carry you home on His shoulders.

Maybe you've wandered. Maybe you drifted. Maybe you chased something that looked good but led you into places you never intended to go. Maybe you feel far. Maybe your heart feels cold or confused. But hear this clearly: Jesus has not stopped calling your name. Not once. And the moment you turn, even slightly, He is already running toward you.

Dogs do not lose their identity when they wander. They do not stop belonging. And neither do you. You are loved, sought after, and welcomed. Every time.

Curl Up Close and Pray

Lord Jesus, thank You for calling me when I wander. Thank You for seeking me out when I drift, for pursuing me with a love that never grows weary, and for welcoming me home every time I turn toward You. Help me hear Your voice above every distraction. Draw my heart back quickly when I stray. Hold me close, Shepherd of my soul, and carry me with the same joy You described, the joy of finding what was lost. Amen.

- 24 –
The Lost Dog

Paws and Open Your Heart

There are few moments more heartbreaking for a dog owner than discovering that your dog is truly lost, not just wandered a little too far in the yard, not momentarily distracted by a squirrel, but gone. Missing. Out of sight. Out of reach. The kind of missing that makes your voice tighten when you call their name. The kind that makes you step off the porch and scan the road with rising anxiety. The kind that sends your heart dropping straight into your stomach. One moment everything is ordinary, predictable, calm. The next moment there is an empty yard, an open gate, or a hole dug under the fence you never noticed before. And suddenly the world feels too big, too dangerous, too unfamiliar for your beloved companion who depends on you for everything.

When a dog is truly lost, you feel it in your whole body. You call their name louder. You walk farther. You check the places they usually love. The hedge line. The wooded trail. The neighbor's yard. The old oak tree. You whistle until your throat hurts. You retrace steps. You circle blocks. You ask neighbors. You shake treat bags. You listen for the faintest bark or whimper or pawstep. Hope rises and falls in waves. Every distant sound makes you freeze and listen harder. Every moving shadow makes you squint. Every car that passes makes your fear tighten, because you know your dog does not understand the dangers of the world the way you do.

Meanwhile, the lost dog is usually not boldly adventuring. They are almost always confused, unsure, frightened, disoriented. The freedom that tempted them loses all appeal once they can no longer see home. They don't understand why the familiar scents are fading or why the road looks strange. They don't know which way leads back to you. Their ears perk at every noise. Their tail lowers. Their confidence melts. They begin wandering with nervous uncertainty, circling, stopping, backtracking. They pause often, listening for your voice, hoping the breeze carries the sound they long for.

Sometimes a lost dog tries to find a familiar landmark but ends up drifting farther from home without intending to. Sometimes they hide behind bushes or under porches, frightened by new sounds. Sometimes they pace in circles, torn between instincts that conflict inside them: "Go back," one instinct says, "but which way is back?" Another instinct says, "Stay put," but fear pushes them to move again. Dogs feel lost far more intensely than we realize, because their world is built entirely on proximity, being close to the one they love is their safety, their anchor, their orientation. When that nearness is gone, everything inside them feels unmoored.

And yet, in the middle of the confusion, something beautiful and faithful lives inside the lost dog: the longing for home. It never fades. It never weakens. No matter how scared they feel, they want to return. No matter how far they've gone, they hope you'll come for them. That longing sits deep in their instinct, a steady ache that whispers, "I am not where I belong."

When a lost dog is finally found, the moment is unforgettable. Whether you spot them peeking from behind a shed or hear their bark in the distance or see their shadow appear on the road, something inside you breaks open with joy. You call their name, and their entire body responds instantly. Their tail whips into a frantic blur, their legs run before their mind can catch up, and they come to you with everything in them, ears pinned back, eyes wide with relief, body trembling with the weight of fear finally undone by reunion. They press themselves into you as if trying to merge their fear into your safety, their wandering into your embrace. And in that instant, you are not thinking about the frustration or the worry or the inconvenience. You are thinking only this: "You're home. Thank God you're home."

Because when something you love deeply is lost, nothing matters more than finding it again. And the reunion heals something in both of you.

Scripture to Sink Your Teeth Into

Luke 15:11–24 (AMP), The Parable of the Lost Son
"…while he was still a long way off, his father saw him and was moved with compassion for him, and ran and embraced him and kissed him."

Lesson To Chew On

There are seasons in life when we are not simply distracted or wandering slightly off the path, we are lost. Lost in choices we regret. Lost in emotions we can't control. Lost in bitterness we didn't mean to nurture. Lost in habits that grew stronger than our resolve. Lost in grief. Lost in shame. Lost in spiritual drift we didn't even notice happening until suddenly we look around and whisper, "How did I get here?" We don't always lose our faith entirely; sometimes we just lose our way. The world feels too big. Our hearts feel too small. God feels too far. And like the lost dog who doesn't know which direction leads home, we pace, fret, hide, or attempt to follow instincts that keep failing us.

The beauty of Jesus' story in Luke 15, the lost sheep, the lost coin, and the lost son, is that being lost does not change your value. The sheep was still worth searching for. The coin was still worth sweeping the whole house for. The son was still worth waiting for. The lostness did not erase worth. It revealed the depth of love. The father didn't wait on the porch tapping his foot, rehearsing lectures. He ran. He embraced. He celebrated. Because love doesn't fixate on how long the wandering lasted. Love rejoices in the moment the lost one turns home.

Being spiritually lost feels terrifying because everything familiar seems far. But God is not like us. He does not get disoriented. He does not lose track of us. He does not panic or worry. He knows exactly where you are, physically, spiritually, emotionally, and He is already moving toward you before you even decide to take one step in His direction. The moment your heart turns, even faintly, toward home, His compassion becomes motion. His mercy becomes pursuit. His grace becomes embrace.

The prodigal son didn't return polished. He didn't return victorious. He didn't return with impressive speeches. He returned broken, dirty, ashamed, rehearsing apologies. But the father stopped his apology mid-sentence. Why? Because the apology wasn't what mattered. The return was. The lostness was over. The reunion had begun. And the father's joy overflowed so loudly that the entire household knew, restoration had come.

You don't have to fix yourself before returning to God. You don't have to clean up your mistakes. You don't have to rebuild all that was broken before you walk toward Him. Lost dogs don't wait until they figure out the right direction; they respond to the voice they recognize. Lost children don't need perfect maps; they need a Father who watches the road.

If you feel lost, in sin, in sorrow, in confusion, in weariness, in spiritual fog, listen for the voice calling you. You may be a long way off, but God has already seen you. He already knows your silhouette on the horizon. And He is not waiting to punish you. He is moving toward you with compassion, with joy, with arms open wide.

Being found does not depend on your ability. It depends on His love.

And when you surrender to that love, when you run, stumble, crawl, or simply turn your heart toward Him, heaven erupts in celebration. Because nothing matters more to God than the moment His lost child comes home.

Curl Up Close and Pray

Lord Jesus, thank You for searching for me when I am lost, for calling my name through the noise of life, and for running toward me long before I take my first step toward You. When I drift, draw me back. When I wander, speak clearly. When I lose my way, remind me that Your love never loses sight of me. Help me trust that no matter how far I go, Your arms remain open and

Your heart remains faithful. Bring me home, Lord, again and again, every time I need You. Amen.

- 25 -
Loyalty in a Lonely World

Paws and Open Your Heart

There is a certain kind of loyalty in dogs that stands out starkly against the loneliness of the world we live in. People drift. Friends change. Crowds move on. Even family relationships shift over time. But a dog's loyalty feels steady in a way that almost startles the human heart. When a dog loves you, it loves you in a way that does not waver with circumstance or mood. The world may be unpredictable, but their devotion is not. Their bond does not depend on your success, your strength, or your emotional state. They do not require explanations or apologies every time life wears you thin. They do not measure you by the day you're having. They simply stay.

It shows in the way they follow you from room to room, not because they need to be entertained, but because their presence is their gift. They lie at your feet while you work, sit beside you while you rest, and walk with you even when you are only pacing through the ordinary corners of the house. Their companionship is subtle but profound. They anchor themselves to you with invisible ties of affection, choosing again and again to be near. Sometimes you may even forget they're in the room until you feel the gentle brush of fur against your leg or glance down to see their quiet eyes watching you with that familiar, reassuring steadiness.

This loyalty becomes even more visible in moments of sadness or loneliness. Dogs have a way of sensing shifts in your spirit before you speak a word. Your sighs, your silence, your slowed steps, they notice these things with a sensitivity that defies explanation. And without demanding anything from you, they draw closer. A chin resting on your knee. A head pressed against your hand. A warm body curled beside you, offering comfort simply by being there. They do not try to fix your sorrow. They do not offer advice. They do not grow uncomfortable with your tears. They simply exist beside you, present and steady, letting their companionship speak for itself.

And their loyalty does not weaken when the world feels heavy. In fact, that's when it shines brightest. A dog does not turn away when you're discouraged or irritable. They do not leave when the house feels quiet or your heart feels tired. They do not retreat when life feels complicated. Their loyalty is not seasonal or circumstantial. It is constant, a steady, living reminder that you are not alone.

What makes this even more remarkable is how freely they give such devotion. They do not weigh the consequences. They do not ask whether you've earned it. Their love operates through instinct, an instinct that binds them to the one they trust. And if you've ever returned home after a long day, worn thin by the noise of the world, and been greeted by a dog whose tail beats like a joyful drum, you know the comfort of that loyalty. It melts something in you. It reminds you that you matter. It pulls you out of the isolation you didn't even realize you were sinking into.

Perhaps one of the most beautiful expressions of a dog's loyalty appears in how they wait. When you leave the house, they do not know where you're going or how long you'll be gone, but they trust you to return. They wait without resentment or fear. They wait with belief. They wait with love. And when you walk back through the door, all the loneliness disappears in an instant under the weight of their joy. Because for them, your presence fills every empty place inside them.

In a lonely world, a dog's loyalty is more than companionship, it is a glimpse of the kind of steadfast love we all long for. It is a quiet sermon in fur and paws, reminding us that love can be unwavering, presence can be healing, and loyalty can still exist in the midst of shifting seasons and uncertain days.

Scripture to Sink Your Teeth Into

Proverbs 18:24 (AMP)
"There is a friend who sticks closer than a brother."

Lesson To Chew On

Loyalty is one of the most powerful expressions of love. It is the glue that holds relationships together through changing seasons, disappointments, hardships, and uncertainties. In a world where people often drift away when things get difficult, the loyalty of a dog stands out like a lighthouse in the fog. It reminds us of the way God loves His children, faithfully, consistently, and without the fear of abandonment. But more than that, a dog's loyalty gives us a picture of the kind of faithfulness God wants to produce in us.

The proverb that describes a friend who "sticks closer than a brother" is ultimately pointing beyond human relationships. It reflects the heart of Jesus, the One who never leaves, never forsakes, never withdraws, never grows tired of our weakness, and never distances Himself when life becomes messy. Jesus is the companion who remains when others walk away, the friend who stays when others grow distant, the Shepherd who guards when others forget. His loyalty is not fragile. It is not conditional. It does not fluctuate with our moods, our mistakes, or our circumstances. It is rooted in the eternal, unchanging love of God.

Many of us know what it feels like to be surrounded by people yet still feel alone. We know what it feels like when friendships fade, when family feels distant, when seasons shift, when people disappoint us, or when relationships fracture in painful ways. Loneliness is not just the absence of people, it is the absence of connection, the absence of steady companionship, the absence of someone who stays. But Jesus stays. He stays in every valley, every storm, every midnight hour, every fragile moment. His loyalty is not symbolic, it is real, felt, lived, and proven over and over again.

The loyalty of Jesus also calls us into a deeper kind of life. Dogs do not offer partial loyalty. They offer whole-hearted devotion. They stay when things are calm, and they stay when things are chaotic. They stay when you are at your best, and they stay when you are at your lowest. That kind of loyalty reflects the heart God wants to shape in us, a loyalty that loves people consistently, that stands beside others without abandoning them in their struggles, that remains present even when it's inconvenient or difficult. Followers of Jesus are called to be people who stay, people who love deeply, people who reflect the faithfulness of the One they follow.

But loyalty also means trusting God with the lonely places in our lives. Sometimes we struggle to believe anyone will stay with us. We fear abandonment. We brace ourselves for rejection. We hesitate to trust because our hearts have been bruised in the past. Yet Jesus invites us not only to trust His loyalty but to rest in it. His presence fills the empty places. His closeness quiets the anxious places. His companionship softens the hurting places. If a dog's presence can bring comfort in loneliness, imagine what the abiding presence of Jesus can do in the soul that welcomes Him.

Loyalty in a lonely world is more than a desire, it is a promise God offers His children. He does not simply send comfort. He is the comfort. He does not simply promise presence. He provides presence. He does not simply tell us we are not alone. He ensures we never will be. And when we learn to walk through life anchored in the loyalty of Christ, we discover a courage we could not find anywhere else.

The loyalty of a dog is a soft echo of a louder truth, the everlasting faithfulness of God. And when we let that truth settle deeply in our hearts, loneliness loses its power. For wherever Jesus is, companionship lives, comfort breathes, and loyalty remains unbroken.

Curl Up Close and Pray

Lord Jesus, thank You for being the Friend who never leaves, the Savior who never abandons, and the Shepherd who stays near in every season. Teach my heart to trust Your loyalty more deeply, to rest in Your presence, and to reflect Your faithfulness in the way I love others. Help me become a person who stays, who cares, who supports, and who loves with the steady devotion that comes from You. When loneliness whispers, let Your voice be louder. When fear tells me I am alone, let Your presence remind me that I am not. Thank You for Your unwavering love. Amen.

- 26 -
The Dog Who Knows Your Voice

Paws and Open Your Heart

There is something remarkable about the way a dog responds to your voice, not just to the sound, but to the soul inside it. Long before they understand words, they understand tone. Long before they recognize commands, they recognize comfort. Long before they can interpret meaning, they can interpret love. A dog knows your voice the way a child knows the sound of their mother's heartbeat, instinctively, intimately, unquestioningly. That voice becomes a lifeline, a compass, a home they can hear even from a distance.

Picture a dog asleep on the couch, curled in a warm little knot of peace. The moment you whisper their name, their ears twitch, their head lifts, and their eyes blink open with recognition. It doesn't matter if they were in the deepest nap imaginable, your voice pulls them gently back into the waking world. Or imagine being outside where distractions, scents, and movement flood their senses. Yet the second you call their name, something inside them snaps to attention. Their body freezes, their ears rotate like little satellites, and they turn toward you with an eagerness that says, "That's the one I love. That sound belongs to me."

Dogs recognize their owner's voice above all others, even in a noisy room. They can ignore dozens of sounds, but not the voice they trust. Even when they wander too far at the park, the moment they hear that familiar tone, they abandon every distraction and run full-speed toward it as though the rest of the world no longer exists. The world may be big, but their heart is tethered to one voice.

What makes this connection even more extraordinary is that dogs respond not just to commands but to emotion. Say a dog's name with joy, and they light up like a lantern. Say it with sadness, and they approach slowly, gently, offering comfort. Say it with a whisper, and they draw near as if closing the distance could close the ache in your voice. They know the difference between laughter and frustration, excitement and grief, playfulness and pain. They hear not only the sound, they hear the heart. A dog's ears are tuned to affection.

There's a beautiful security in that. Knowing your voice anchors them. It orients them. It reassures them. They may be anxious, pacing the room during a thunderstorm, trembling at the cracks of lightning. But your voice, even a soft, steady murmur, begins to slow their breathing. Fear loosens its grip. Their body eases. They move closer until they can feel your presence. Because for them, your voice is not merely a signal. It is safety.

Dogs also distinguish between the voice of their owner and the voice of strangers. A stranger may call their name, but the dog hesitates. They look back at you for reassurance. They check your expression. They listen for your instruction. They need your confirmation before they respond to anyone else. Your voice is the anchor point by which all other sounds are judged.

And perhaps the most tender moment of all is when you come home after being away. You say their name while opening the door, just one word, spoken with affection, and the house instantly erupts with joy. Their nails tap the floor like a rapid drumbeat. Their tail slaps the air in wild loops. Their whole body wiggles with delight. They heard you coming long before they saw you. And your voice was all it took to awaken joy inside them.

We rarely think about how powerful our voice is to our dogs. But they carry it inside them like a familiar melody, a song that means home. Through distractions, noise, storms, fear, or distance, they know your voice. And knowing it changes everything for them.

Scripture to Sink Your Teeth Into

John 10:27 (AMP)
"My sheep hear My voice, and I know them, and they follow Me."

Lesson To Chew On

We live in a world filled with voices, loud ones, persuasive ones, persistent ones, deceptive ones, discouraging ones. Voices that tell us we're not enough. Voices that pull us toward compromise. Voices that stir fear or anxiety. Voices that distract us with noise. Voices that echo old wounds. Voices that promise fulfillment but deliver emptiness. And sometimes, if we are honest, we follow these voices simply because they are present, immediate, or familiar. We begin to forget which voice truly leads us home.

But Jesus says, "My sheep hear My voice... and they follow Me." He is not describing an occasional recognition. He is describing a relationship, the same kind of deep, instinctual, trust-filled recognition a dog has when hearing its owner. Jesus speaks to His children through Scripture, through the Spirit, through worship, through conviction, through peace, through wisdom, through the quiet nudges of the heart. His voice carries a tone you won't find anywhere else: truth without cruelty, correction without condemnation, love without condition, strength without intimidation, guidance without pressure.

Many believers struggle with discerning God's voice not because He isn't speaking, but because the world is loud. It fills our minds with constant noise. It bombards us with information, opinions, temptations, and distractions. And like a dog listening to dozens of sounds at once, we sometimes lose focus. But when we tune our ears to Jesus, really tune, we begin to recognize Him with growing clarity. His voice stands apart. His tone is unmistakable. His words, whether whispered into our spirit or read in Scripture, create peace, not confusion. They draw us closer, not push us away. They align with truth, not distort it.

A dog never mistakes the voice of a stranger for the voice of its owner. And God desires that same clarity in us. When temptations call our name, when fear shouts lies, when anxiety fills our thoughts, when worldly voices entice us with empty promises, the Shepherd's voice cuts through the noise: "This is the way. Walk in it." And something inside the believer's heart recognizes the difference. The closer we stay to Jesus, the quicker we discern His voice.

But just like a dog who wanders too far may struggle to hear clearly, believers who drift from closeness with God often find His voice faint. Not because He stopped speaking, but because distance dulls discernment. That is why staying near the Shepherd, through prayer, Scripture, worship, fellowship, and obedience, matters so deeply. Nearness shapes recognition. Recognition shapes obedience. Obedience shapes safety. The more we stay close, the less the noise of the world can pull us away.

There is also comfort in knowing that Jesus knows our voice too. We call to Him in fear, and He responds. We whisper prayers in weakness, and He hears. We cry out in desperation, and He moves. The relationship is mutual: He calls, and we follow, and we call, and He answers. The Shepherd is not distant; He is attentive.

A dog runs toward the voice of its owner because it is the

sound of love. In the same way, the Christian heart is wired to come alive when it hears the voice of God. That voice is our safety, our compass, our anchor, our comfort, and our home. When we learn to recognize it, truly recognize it, everything in our spiritual life changes. The noise loses its power. Temptation loses its grip. Fear loses its volume. Confusion loses its influence.

Because the voice of Jesus is the one voice that leads us to life.

Curl Up Close and Pray

Lord Jesus, teach me to discern Your voice above every noise around me. Quiet the world, calm my heart, and soften my spirit so I can hear You clearly. Help me stay close to You so that when You speak, through Scripture, through conviction, through peace, my heart responds without hesitation. Make Your voice familiar, comforting, unmistakable to me. And when fear, temptation, or confusion tries to call my name, let me recognize instantly that it is not You. Shepherd, speak, and I will follow. Amen.

- 27 -
When They Won't Let Go of the Leash

Paws and Open Your Heart

There is a certain tug-of-war every dog owner has experienced, that moment when a dog sinks its teeth into the leash and refuses to let go. It doesn't matter that the leash was designed to guide them, not entertain them. It doesn't matter that biting it turns a peaceful walk into a clumsy parade of sideways shuffling and awkward pulling. In that moment, the leash becomes an object of stubborn determination. Some dogs bite it because they're excited; they can't wait to go somewhere, and holding the leash feels like they're participating. Others clamp down because they want control, they want to decide the pace, direction, or timing. And others bite it simply because something in their playful spirit says, "This seems fun. Why not?"

If you've ever tried to walk a dog who refuses to release the leash, you know how ridiculous the scene becomes. You tug gently, trying not to hurt their mouth. They tug back, thinking it's a game. You step forward, and they step sideways. You pause, hoping they'll drop it, and they brace their body as if preparing for a wrestling match. You try distraction, a treat, a toy, a kind word, but the dog is determined. That leash is theirs now, and they intend to keep it. What started as a peaceful walk becomes a slow, stumbling dance of competing wills.

From the outside, it looks funny, even endearing. But from the inside, especially when you're running late or trying to keep pace, it becomes frustrating. Not because you're angry at the dog, but because you know something they don't. You know where the walk is headed. You know the safe path and the dangerous areas. You know where the cars pass, where the uneven ground lies, where the other dogs bark behind fences. You know how long the walk should last, where the water bowl awaits, and how far their little paws should travel before they become tired. You see the whole picture, but your dog only sees the moment, and in the moment, they're convinced the leash belongs in their mouth.

Sometimes, as you gently tug to regain control, you catch their eyes. Behind all the stubbornness, the mischief, the determination, there is trust. They don't cling to the leash because they doubt your love. They cling because they're excited, impatient, or unaware. They want to move faster than they should, or in a direction that isn't right, or with a pace their body can't sustain. But even in their stubborn grip, they stay close. They don't run off with the leash into the woods. They don't disappear. They stay beside you, tugging, resisting, testing, but still yours.

There's something tender about that. Even in their refusal to let go, their heart is still turned toward you. Their stubbornness is wrapped in affection. They don't trust themselves with the world around them; they trust you. They just don't trust you enough in that moment to let you lead. And yet, even in their tugging, they never leave your side.

Eventually, after the pulling and negotiating, after the playful wrestling and determined grip, there comes a moment when they finally release the leash. Maybe they get tired of holding it. Maybe something more interesting catches their attention. Maybe your voice softens their will. Or maybe they finally understand that walking goes better when they're not dragging the leash sideways. But the moment they release it, the entire walk changes. The tension eases. Their steps fall into rhythm with yours. Their head lifts. Their body relaxes. They begin to enjoy what was meant to be enjoyed all along, the companionship, the movement, the fresh air, the freedom that comes from trusting the one who guides them.

Watching a dog let go of the leash is a small, everyday picture of a much deeper truth hiding inside the human heart.

Scripture to Sink Your Teeth Into

Psalm 32:8 (AMP)
"I will instruct you and teach you in the way you should go; I

will counsel you [who are willing to learn] with My eye upon you."

Lesson To Chew On

There is a part of the human soul that behaves just like a dog who won't let go of the leash. We hold onto control with our teeth clenched tightly around our plans, our timing, our desires, our expectations, our fears, our habits, our assumptions about what should happen and how it should happen. We grip the "leash" because we want to feel secure, or because we fear the unknown, or because we are convinced that if we stop controlling everything, things will fall apart. And like the dog determined to steer the walk, we often end up creating tension, confusion, and exhaustion, not because God is harsh or controlling, but because we cannot fully enjoy the path while fighting the One who knows it best.

We do this in our relationships, trying to orchestrate outcomes. We do it with our children, gripping tightly to their decisions and futures. We do it with our finances, careers, ministries, and personal dreams, clinging to the illusion that we can manage everything on our own. We do it in moments of fear, where controlling the leash feels safer than releasing it. We do it in moments of impatience, where God's timing feels too slow. We do it in seasons of uncertainty, gripping harder when God invites us to trust deeper.

But Psalm 32:8 reveals God's heart: "I will instruct you and teach you in the way you should go… with My eye upon you." God does not lead from a distance. He walks beside us, His hand steady on the leash, His gaze attentive, His presence constant. He knows the terrain ahead of us. He knows the safe paths and the dangerous ones. He knows the valleys where our strength will fail and the mountaintops where our perspective will widen. He knows when we need rest and when we need courage. He knows the timing that protects us and the steps that prepare us. He knows the journey in full, while we only see the next few feet.

Yet even knowing all that, God does not rip the leash from our mouths. He does not drag us or scold us or give up on us. He is patient. He is kind. He waits for us to release control willingly. He whispers gently to our hearts. He tugs lightly in the right direction. He walks at our pace, even when our stubbornness slows the journey. And when we finally let go, when we surrender the illusion of control, something shifts inside us. Peace replaces tension. Joy replaces frustration. Trust replaces anxiety. The walk becomes smoother, not because the terrain changed, but because our posture did.

Letting go of the leash does not mean losing freedom; it means gaining direction. It means stepping into sync with the God who sees what we cannot. It means experiencing the journey with far more joy than when we are fighting against Him. The miracles happen, the clarity becomes real, and the path unfolds when we stop tugging and start trusting.

And perhaps the most beautiful part of all is this: even when we don't let go right away, God never lets go of His end. He doesn't abandon us. He doesn't walk away frustrated. He stays close. He stays steady. He stays faithful. Because for Him, the walk is not about perfection, it is about relationship. It is about being with us. It is about leading us safely, lovingly, patiently toward the place He has prepared for us.

Dogs eventually learn that the walk becomes better when they release the leash. And our spiritual lives become fuller, richer, and freer when we do the same. Letting go is not losing control. Letting go is choosing trust. It is choosing God's wisdom over our own. It is choosing His pace over our urgency. It is choosing His direction over our instincts. It is choosing closeness with Him over the stubbornness that keeps us from enjoying the journey.

Curl Up Close and Pray

Lord Jesus, I confess that I often hold onto the leash of my own life with a stubborn grip. Help me release control, trust Your guidance, and walk in step with You instead of wrestling against You. Teach me to surrender my plans, my fears, my timing, and my expectations into Your loving hands. Thank You for Your patience, Your kindness, and Your steady presence. Lead me, Lord. I will follow. Amen.

- 28 -

Sitting at Your Feet

Paws and Open Your Heart

There is a quiet, sacred beauty in the way a dog chooses to sit at your feet. It is not dramatic. It is not loud. It is not attention-seeking. It is simple, steady, and deeply affectionate. A dog's decision to settle by your feet speaks of trust, comfort, closeness, and a desire to be near without demanding anything from you. They sit there whether you are working at a desk, reading in a chair, watching television, or resting at the end of a long day. Their nearness is not about needing entertainment, it is about relationship. They feel safe when they are close. They feel connected when they are near. To them, your feet are not just a place to rest; they are a place to belong.

Dogs are drawn to their owner's presence in a way that feels instinctively spiritual. They sense your movements, your moods, the rhythm of your steps, the tone of your breath. They know when you are relaxed and when you are burdened. They can tell when you are focused or when you are tired. And when they choose to sit at your feet, it is their way of saying, "I'm here. I don't need anything. I just want to be close to you." That kind of closeness is rare in human relationships, closeness without expectation, presence without performance.

Sometimes a dog sits at your feet in perfect stillness, curled into a peaceful ball of fur, content simply to share your space. They breathe slowly and deeply, letting your nearness calm whatever tension or leftover energy flickers inside them. Other times, they sit alert, eyes watching you with a mixture of admiration and curiosity. They study your face, your hands, your patterns, as if trying to understand you more. And then there are times when they sit at your feet because they sense something is off within you. They lean into your leg or rest their head gently across your foot, offering silent companionship that says more than words ever could.

What makes this simple act so meaningful is that a dog could be anywhere else. They could be on a soft cushion, stretched across the couch, exploring the house, or chasing something in the yard. But instead, they choose your feet, the place closest to your presence. It is not glamorous. It is not elevated. It is not comfortable in the same way a warm blanket or soft dog bed might be. But to them, sitting beside you is better than lying somewhere luxurious alone. Their peace is connected to your proximity.

There is humility, devotion, and love wrapped into that simple posture. Dogs don't sit at your feet because they feel small; they sit there because they feel safe. They don't sit there because they have nothing better to do; they sit there because you are what is better. And every time they do, they remind us of the kind of closeness the human soul longs for, the longing to be near someone who loves us, someone who cares for us, someone who understands us, someone whose presence makes us feel at peace.

If you've ever reached down absentmindedly to stroke a dog sitting by your feet, you've felt the warmth of that bond. The gentle movement of your hand, the softening of their eyes, the relaxation of their body, it's a quiet exchange of affection that needs no explanation. They don't require your full attention; your presence is enough. They don't demand anything of you; being near you is the gift. And sometimes, when the world feels uncertain or overwhelming, that faithful presence at your feet can be unexpectedly comforting. It whispers, "You're not alone. I'm here. I choose to be near you."

There is something holy about that kind of nearness, because it mirrors a deeper longing woven into the human heart, the longing to sit at the feet of the One who loves us most.

Scripture to Sink Your Teeth Into

Luke 10:38–39 (AMP)
"…Mary, who seated herself at the Lord's feet and was continually listening to His teaching."

Lesson To Chew On

There is a profound spiritual truth hidden in the simple image of a dog sitting at your feet. It mirrors the posture of Mary in Luke 10, the woman who chose something far greater than busyness, productivity, or performance. While Martha hurried around the house, distracted by preparations, Mary sat at Jesus's feet, listening, resting, receiving. She was not lazy. She was not indifferent to responsibility. She simply understood that there is a time to work and a time to be still, and being still in the presence of Jesus was not wasted time; it was holy time.

Too often, we treat our relationship with God like Martha treated her household tasks. We rush. We worry. We multitask. We strive, plan, and push, believing that value comes from what we accomplish rather than who we sit with. We check our spiritual boxes, a quick prayer here, a hurried devotion there, but our souls remain restless because we haven't truly stopped. We haven't been still. We haven't sat at His feet.

Sitting at Jesus's feet is not about inactivity, it is about intimacy. It is about choosing presence over productivity, relationship over routine, connection over commotion. It is about positioning ourselves close enough to hear His voice, sense His nearness, and receive His love without rushing. Spiritual strength is not built in frantic motion; it is built in quiet proximity.

Like the dog who sits peacefully at your feet, our souls long for nearness to the One who brings us security, comfort, direction, and rest. God never forces us to sit. He does not drag us into stillness. He invites. He whispers. He nudges. But the choice to draw near is ours. And when we choose closeness, real closeness, something inside us finally exhales.

When we sit at Jesus's feet, our anxious thoughts begin to quiet. Our frantic pace slows. Our burdens feel lighter. Our fears lose their power. His words begin to reshape our thoughts. His presence resets our priorities. His love rewrites our sense of worth. We become like Mary, not worried about many things, because our hearts have discovered the one thing that truly matters.

Sitting at Jesus's feet doesn't mean abandoning responsibility. It means grounding yourself in His presence so that everything you do flows from a place of peace instead of pressure. It means letting His voice guide your decisions, His love fuel your actions, His wisdom shape your steps. It means returning again and again to the place where your soul finds its true home.

The world will always try to pull you away. Distractions will always clamor for your attention. Demands will always shout for priority. But Jesus gently continues to offer the same invitation He offered Mary: "Come sit with Me." Not because He needs your company, but because you need His.

Dogs sit at their owner's feet because they know where they belong. They know where they are safe. They know where their heart feels at rest. Your soul knows the same truth. It knows that the safest, truest, most life-giving place is at the feet of Jesus.

To sit at His feet is to choose relationship over rushing. To choose peace over pressure. To choose nearness over noise. It is the sacred decision, repeated daily, to be close to the One whose presence changes everything.

Curl Up Close and Pray

Lord Jesus, draw my heart back to Your feet. Teach me to choose closeness over busyness, stillness over striving, and intimacy with You over the noise that fills my days. Quiet my spirit. Settle my thoughts. Let me hear Your voice clearly and rest in Your presence deeply. Help me return again and again to the place where my soul feels safe and my heart feels whole, right at Your feet. Amen.

- 29 -
The Dog Waiting for a Treat

Paws and Open Your Heart

There's a special kind of anticipation a dog has when it knows a treat is coming. It doesn't matter if it's a small biscuit, a soft chew, or even a tiny piece of chicken, once that dog senses a reward in the air, its entire body becomes a picture of eager expectation. The ears perk straight up, the eyes widen with bright attention, the tail sweeps back and forth like a metronome gone wild, and the body shifts from paw to paw as if it can barely contain the joy bubbling inside. Dogs don't hide their excitement. They don't pretend to be calm. They don't mask their hunger. They simply live fully, openly, honestly in the moment, filled with childlike delight at the good thing they believe is coming.

What makes it even more endearing is how a dog waits when it knows the treat depends on obedience. You say "Sit," and they drop to the ground instantly, maybe a little crooked, maybe a little shaky, but fully committed. You say "Stay," and their whole body vibrates with restraint, every muscle longing to spring forward but held in place by love and desire to please. Their eyes lock onto the treat in your hand with laser focus, and yet, every few seconds, those eyes flick upward to your face as if to say, "I'm doing it! I'm being good! I trust you! Is it time yet?"

And then there is the unmistakable joy of the reward itself. The moment you say the word, "Okay!", or extend your hand toward them, they burst into motion with a happiness no human could ever fake. Their tail becomes a blur, their paws scramble, and they receive the treat with an enthusiasm that turns even a tiny snack into a celebration. It doesn't matter how small the gift is. What matters is who it came from. To them, the treat is a tangible expression of love, an act of connection, a sign that their obedience was seen and valued.

But one of the most touching parts of this little ritual is what happens even before the treat appears. A dog's expectation begins long before the smell reaches them or the package crinkles. They begin hoping simply because of your movements, your tone, your routine, your patterns. They learn the sound of the cabinet where the treats are stored, the way your hand moves toward the pocket where you sometimes keep rewards, the gentle shift in your voice when you're about to give them something good. Dogs develop an intuition for blessing. They can sense goodness on its way.

Even when they don't understand the timing, they trust the character of the giver. Even when the treat doesn't come instantly, their hope doesn't disappear. They may wiggle. They may whine softly. They may inch closer with bright eyes and lifted eyebrows. But they stay expectant. They wait with a joyful kind of surrender, not anxious, not panicked, not discouraged, but believing that something good is coming because the one who loves them is preparing it.

What a beautiful thing it is to be watched like that, with eyes that know you are kind, hands that give generously, and a heart that wouldn't withhold what would bless them. A dog's eagerness isn't rooted in entitlement; it's rooted in trust. They trust you to give them good things. They trust you to do what's best. They trust your timing more than they understand it. And in their waiting, their patient, hopeful waiting, you catch a glimpse of something profoundly spiritual.

Because that kind of anticipation, that quiet confidence that something good is coming, is the posture the human heart was meant to have toward God.

Scripture to Sink Your Teeth Into

Psalm 62:5 (AMP)
"For God alone my soul waits in silence and quietly submits to Him, for my hope is from Him."

Lesson To Chew On

Waiting is one of the most challenging spiritual disciplines, not because God is silent, but because our hearts are impatient. We want answers now. Breakthrough now. Healing now. Provision now. Change now. The waiting feels uncomfortable, and in that discomfort, we sometimes grow restless or discouraged. Yet Scripture invites us into a different kind of waiting, the kind that looks more like the joyful anticipation of a dog waiting for a treat than the anxious fear humans often carry.

Psalm 62:5 says, "For God alone my soul waits… for my hope is from Him." Notice that waiting and hope are inseparable. The psalmist isn't waiting with dread; he's waiting with confidence. He isn't waiting for an outcome; he's waiting for a Person. He isn't hoping in his own ability; he's hoping in God's character. This changes everything.

A dog waits for a treat not because it doubts whether the treat will come, but because it trusts the one who gives it. In the same way, the believer's waiting becomes peaceful when our trust shifts from the outcome to the One who orchestrates it. God's timing is not a punishment. It is protection. It is preparation. It is perfection. He gives good gifts, always, but He gives them at the right time.

Many times, our spiritual frustration comes from looking at the "treat" rather than the "giver." We fix our eyes on the blessing we want instead of the God who blesses. We try to force the timing, like a dog who tries to jump early and ends up stumbling over its own excitement. But when we fix our eyes on God instead of the thing we want from Him, we discover a deeper peace. The question shifts from "When will God give me what I want?" to "How can I stay close to the God I trust?"

There is also something beautiful about obedience tied to expectation. A dog sits, stays, waits, and behaves not out of fear but out of love. Its obedience is joyful, rooted in relationship. God desires the same from us. Some blessings are attached to obedience not because God is transactional but because He is wise. He knows that certain gifts would harm us if we received them prematurely. He knows that blessings given too early become burdens. He knows that promises fulfilled without preparation become pitfalls. And so He teaches us to sit. To stay. To trust. To obey. Not to earn His love, we already have that, but to grow into the version of ourselves that can receive what He longs to give.

A dog's expectancy is also full of pleasure. They enjoy waiting because they know goodness is coming. Imagine how different our lives would feel if we waited that way, if expectation replaced anxiety, if hope replaced fear, if trust replaced impatience. What if we believed, deeply and sincerely, that God was preparing something good, even when we couldn't see it? What if we trusted His timing enough to stay still, stay faithful, and stay near?

Waiting becomes worship when we believe the Giver is good.

And here is the final truth dogs teach us: they don't need big treats to feel big joy. A tiny biscuit can turn their whole day into a celebration. The same is true for those who walk closely with God. When our hearts are aligned with Him, even the smallest blessings feel enormous, a whisper of peace, a moment of clarity, a gentle encouragement, an unexpected provision, a door quietly opening. And when the larger blessings come, the breakthroughs, the answered prayers, the miracles, our joy becomes complete.

A dog waiting for a treat teaches us how to wait on God: with hope, with trust, with obedience, with joy, and with a heart anchored in the goodness of the One who never fails to give what is best.

Curl Up Close and Pray

Lord Jesus, teach my heart to wait for You with joyful expectation. Replace my anxiety with hope, my impatience with trust, and my worry with quiet confidence in Your goodness. Help me obey with love, not fear, believing that You are preparing good things for me. Make me attentive to Your voice and patient with Your timing. I trust You, Lord, not just for Your blessings, but for who You are. Amen.

- 30 -
The Dog No One Wanted

Paws and Open Your Heart

There are some dogs whose stories break your heart long before you ever meet them. Dogs who have lived through things they never should have endured. Dogs who have felt the sting of a hand that should have protected them. Dogs who have known hunger, fear, neglect, and loneliness in ways that leave permanent marks, on their bodies and on their souls. These are the dogs no one wants at first glance. They're too afraid, too scarred, too broken, too "complicated." They look rough around the edges, and for many people, that's enough reason to pass by their kennel without ever learning who they truly are.

Imagine a dog like that, thin from lack of food, ribs showing through patchy fur. His eyes carry the kind of sadness that only comes from betrayal. His tail curls tightly underneath him as if trying to protect the little hope he has left. He flinches at sudden movements. He doesn't expect kindness, because kindness has never been his experience. Somewhere along the line he was hit, yelled at, starved, abandoned. Somewhere along the line, the ones who should have cared for him walked out and never looked back.

And now he finds himself behind cold metal bars in a concrete kennel, deep in the back corner of an overcrowded pound. Dogs bark constantly around him, but he hardly responds. He simply curls up, waiting for whatever comes next. The volunteers do their best, but he's shut down, too afraid to trust, too wounded to hope. People walk through the shelter and glance into his kennel, but no one stops. No one kneels down. No one sees worth in him. He is "the difficult one." "The damaged one." "The one no one can help." The one at the very bottom of the adoption list.

And as the days pass, his situation becomes more dire. The shelter is full. New dogs arrive every day, cute puppies, friendly dogs, healthy dogs, happy dogs, dogs that people want. But him? He is considered "unadoptable." His name is placed on a list that no dog should ever be on, a list that determines who will be held… and who will be put down. Death row. A term that sounds harsh because it is. It's the final stop for the dogs who have run out of time, out of options, and out of hope.

That dog curls into a tight ball on the blanket they gave him, not because it is warm, but because it is the only comfort he has left. The world has told him one message again and again:

"You're not wanted." And he believes it. He doesn't lift his head when people pass by anymore. He doesn't bark for attention. He doesn't beg for affection. His hope, once flickering, is now nearly gone.

But then something happens, something unexpected. Someone comes in who isn't looking for a perfect dog. Someone who isn't impressed by a wagging tail or a cheerful bark. Someone whose eyes notice the dog others overlook. This person doesn't walk past his kennel like the rest. Instead, they stop. They kneel. They look past the scars, past the fear, past the trembling shoulders and lowered eyes, and they see something else, value. Worth. Potential. Beauty. A soul deserving love.

They speak softly at first, and the dog doesn't move. But the voice keeps coming, gentle, patient, kind. A hand appears quietly at the bars, not forcing anything, just offering presence. A treat is placed near him. A soothing word follows. And for the first time in a long time, the dog lifts his eyes. Just barely. Just enough to see that someone stayed. Someone chose him.

And then, the miracle moment, the kennel door opens. Slowly. Carefully. Intentionally. They put a leash on him. They whisper words of hope. And before he fully understands what is happening, he is led away from the place of death. Led away from the finality that awaited him. Led away from the life he once knew. He doesn't know why he was chosen. He doesn't know what he did to deserve salvation. But he knows one thing: he was rescued. Not because of his goodness. Not because he earned it. Not because he was the best choice. But because someone loved him enough to save him.

Every scar, every wound, every fear he carried does not make his new owner love him less, it makes the rescue more beautiful. And as he takes each tentative step into a new life, he begins to understand something life-changing:

He was wanted all along. He just needed the right Master to see him.

Scripture to Sink Your Teeth Into

Luke 19:10 (AMP)
"For the Son of Man has come to seek and to save that which was lost."

Lesson To Chew On

There is a sacred and unmistakable parallel between that abandoned dog on death row and the story of every human heart apart from Christ. Whether we realize it or not, every one of us has been the dog no one wanted at some point, not by God, but by this broken world. Life has a way of wounding us, scarring us, breaking us down, and convincing us we are too damaged, too sinful, too far gone for grace. Some people carry emotional scars from abuse. Some carry shame from choices they regret. Some carry burdens they don't speak about. Some feel unlovable because of their past. Some believe their mistakes have disqualified them from being wanted by anyone, especially God.

Like that dog in the shelter, humanity is not simply "misplaced", it is lost. Separated. Broken. Afraid. The Bible doesn't hide this truth. It doesn't sugarcoat our condition. Scripture says we were "dead in our sins," trapped in a spiritual prison we could never escape on our own. We were not wandering puppies needing direction, we were condemned sinners needing rescue. Our kennel was the darkness of our own sin. Our chains were guilt, fear, pride, and rebellion. And the worst part? We could not fix ourselves. We couldn't escape. We couldn't earn forgiveness. We couldn't clean ourselves up. We were spiritually on death row, awaiting a judgment we had fully earned.

But then, just like the rescuer who walked into that shelter, Jesus came.

He didn't come looking for the strongest or the prettiest or the best behaved. He didn't come to collect the deserving. He didn't walk by the brokenhearted. He didn't ignore the fearful. He didn't overlook the scarred. Scripture says He came to seek and to save the lost, the bruised, the wounded, the ashamed, the guilty, the people who feel like they aren't worth saving. Jesus didn't come for the "adoptable." He came for the hopeless. He came for the condemned. He came for the ones who had run out of time and ran out of chances.

He entered the "shelter" of this world, its darkness, its brokenness, its cruelty, and He walked straight toward the worst of us. Not the best. Not the cleaned-up versions. The real us, scars, wounds, sins, fears, and all. He knelt beside our spiritual kennel, looked us in the eyes, and whispered, "I choose you." Not because you were perfect. Not because you could offer Him something. Not because you were the easiest to love. But because His heart is drawn to the broken. He is the Savior who specializes in the outcasts, the forgotten, the overlooked, the ones who believe they are beyond help.

Jesus opened the door not by pushing metal bars aside but by stretching His arms on a cross. His blood became the signature on your adoption papers. His resurrection became the leash that leads you out of death and into life. And when He takes your trembling soul by the hand, He doesn't pull you out with frustration, He leads you with compassion.

Just like that rescued dog, we don't understand the fullness of the miracle at first. Salvation begins with steps, small, shaky, uncertain. But the One who rescues us does not abandon us halfway. He teaches us to trust. He heals our wounds. He restores our dignity. He gives us a name, a home, a place, a purpose. He replaces fear with belonging. He replaces panic with peace. He replaces loneliness with love. He holds us close when we're afraid, feeds us when we're empty, comforts us when we tremble, and stays with us when the memories of our past try to convince us we're still unwanted.

And perhaps the most beautiful truth of all is this:

Jesus didn't adopt you because no one else wanted you. He adopted you because He wanted you.

You are not God's last pick. You are not an obligation. You are His joy. His treasure. His beloved. The Bible says He came "to seek", meaning He pursued you, and "to save", meaning He rescued you. Salvation is not a reward; it is a rescue. And just like that dog who finds a new life in the arms of a loving master, every believer finds their true home in the arms of Christ.

Curl Up Close and Pray

Lord Jesus, thank You for being the God who came looking for me when I was lost, wounded, afraid, and unable to save myself. Thank You for choosing me even when I felt unworthy, unloved, and unwanted. You saw value in me when I saw none in myself. You opened the door to freedom with Your blood, and You led me out of darkness with Your mercy. Heal the broken places of my heart, restore what sin has damaged, and teach me to walk confidently in the new life You've given me. I am Yours, Lord. Thank You for rescuing me from death and loving me into a life I never knew was possible. Amen.

Paws for Reflection
A Final Wag of Praise

As we come to the close of these 30 devotions in Paws and Praise Jesus, I invite you to pause for a moment and reflect on the journey we've shared. From the exuberant tail-wags of joy that mirror our longing for God's presence to the quiet faithfulness of a dog waiting at the door, echoing the steadfast love of our Savior, each page has been a gentle reminder that God didn't just create dogs as companions; He crafted them as living sermons, preaching truths about His heart in ways words alone could never capture. Think back to Captain Ron's story, that frail puppy rescued from the brink, who became a lineage of love through Wee Dawg and now Lottie. Their lives aren't mere anecdotes; they're parables of redemption, showing us how God takes the broken, the overlooked, and the weary, and transforms them into vessels of joy and purpose. In the same way, these devotions have drawn parallels between muddy paws and mercy, leashes of love and divine guidance, and the simple act of fetching to our pursuit of what truly satisfies. Dogs teach us to trust without seeing the full path, to forgive without holding grudges, to rest in the assurance of a Master's care, and to run home when we've wandered too far. But this book isn't meant to end here, it's an invitation to live it out. Look at your own furry friend today (or remember one from your past) and see them anew: as a divine gift, a daily prompt to draw closer to Jesus. Share these stories with a fellow dog lover, perhaps gifting this book as a seed of encouragement. Let the lessons linger in your prayers, your walks, and your quiet moments, transforming ordinary interactions into sacred encounters with God's grace. As you turn the final page, may your heart be filled with the same unbridled enthusiasm a dog shows its owner, running toward Jesus with abandon, knowing He is the ultimate Home where every stray finds belonging, every wound finds healing, and every soul finds eternal joy. A Final Prayer to Paws and Praise

Heavenly Father,

Thank You for the gift of dogs, these faithful reflections of Your unending love. As we've journeyed through these devotions, stir in us a deeper devotion to You, the Good Shepherd who calls us by name, leads us beside still waters, and restores our souls. Help us to love like they do: wholeheartedly, without reservation, always ready to follow where You lead. May our lives become living testimonies of Your grace, bringing praise to Jesus in every step, every wag, and every faithful day. Amen. And remember, in the grand story of eternity, perhaps we'll see our beloved pets again, bounding toward us in fields of glory, tails wagging in perfect, heavenly joy. Until then, keep praising, keep loving, and keep walking with Him.

Amen

www.ingramcontent.com/pod-product-compliance
Lightning Source LLC
Chambersburg PA
CBHW051838090426
42736CB00011B/1865